ELIANE DA SILVA

VIRGIN MARY:
THE TITLES OF AN UNIQUE WOMAN

1st Edition

GlobalSouth
P R E S S

For more information, please contact info@globalsouthpress.com
or go to http://www.globalsouthpress.com/

Book design by **Héctor Guzmán**
Translated by Larissa Cardoso

Virgin Mary- The Titles of a Unique Woman
By DA SILVA, Eliane—1st ed. — 2016
Library of Congress Control Number: 2015959758
Includes bibliographical references and index.
ISBN: 978-1-943350-22-3

1. Religion studies — Catholicism
2. Christianity — Mariology
3.International Studies — Brazil

RaisingSouth

P R E S S

Editorial Board:

I dedicate this book to my parents, Maria Divina and Ovidio Lucindo (in memoriam), to my dear husband Marcio Oliveira and my beloved daughters, Ayo Makeba and Aissatou Maria.

CONTENT

WHO HAVE NEVER HEARD OF MARY?

AVE! MARIA...
[...] Hail! Mary of the stars, Hail!
Moonlight full of grace, Mary!
Harmony of soft song,
From the heavenly harps bland harmony ...

[...]

The Light! Eucharist beauty,
Sacred flame lit in the Gospel,
Wonder of Love and Sin!

Cruz e Souza (1993)

Besides having the most pronounced name of all time, Mary has titles that make justice to a religiousness that have long been expressed by many people worldwide. Christians and non-Christians, in their innermost instincts, have heard stories of healing and deliverance starring this singular woman.

Our Lady of Conception Aparecida, hold this child! It was the cry of a devoted mother to see her son dying. She was washing clothes in a river stream in the state of Minas Gerais, Brazil. She was holding a baby with one hand and was carrying on the clothes with the other. The child, in an oversight, jumped from her lap and fell into a big hole. By running to help him, she realized that her prayer had been answered. The boy was playing happily without suffering a scratch. I knew about this and several other events which followed the same line, since the woman above was my mother, who experienced and witnessed this and other facts.

Rich and poor have had successful experiences to cling and deliver the problems in the hands of the one considered the intermediary of God. Through novenas, prayers and chants it seems a facilitated approach to the words to reach the ears of God's mother. But why?

The world is lacking love. The people need to feel welcome and safe. There are religious wars, racial prejudice, misogyny and a multitude of horrors happening not only in Brazil but all over the planet. Very often the key to open the door for the winds to take away what it is doing wrong is in the comfort of prayers dedicated to Mary. A woman, like any mother, is considered the one that meets to take care of children.

Have you ever used or may have heard someone use the interjections "Vixe Maria!", "Vixe!", "Ixe!" Virgin Mary "is not it? So these expressions are all corruptions of the noun" Virgin Mary ", which with time, experienced reductions so as to save effort, as with many other words, whether they are in English or in other language. Thus, the term has been reduced to 'virgin' passing 'prevails', 'Vixe' and last 'ixe'.Words used most often in awe of situations scare.

You may have heard many titles given to Jesus' mother, right? Here we will speak of the various epithets given to Mary. There are qualifiers that remember her vocation and mission in relation to Christ and the Church (Mother of the Savior, my Lord's mother); extolling her qualities (Prudent Virgin, Virgin, Noble Lady); some remember certain facts of her life (Our Lady of Sorrows, Our Lady of Mercy); others accept her as a representative of a local place or country (Patron Saint of Brazil, Lady of Latin America); many recall some Virgin's intercession in favor of men (Mother of the poor and weak, Virgin of the Helpless, Mother of mankind); it is also recognized by the beauty and sweetness (kind Mother, beautiful Mother, dear Mother); and so on.

Our Lady of Aparecida, Patroness of Brazil, is placed in evidence and receives special attention in the hymns, which call her too often of "liberating mother of the poor and oppressed", "Mother Aparecida", "Mother of God and ours ".

The Marian texts are defined primarily through the history of Mary and epithets presented in fifty songs selected for analysis; and they have as collaborative aspect the development of a careful selection of hymns, which in turn, were selected from several copies of song books that can be found in many Catholic churches in Brazil [1].

In this work we present the various qualifying terms that were given to Mary; it turns out that a large portion of these treatments are focused on the idea of a liberating Marian image, whose primary function is to care and free the poor and lowly. The many chants disclosed deal practically with topics related to the theme of the Holy liberator, perhaps because they are texts written by Brazilian authors and focused on liberation theology[2], which propagate a reality observed in Brazil, considering that Mary is the holy chosen by a large proportion of religious people.

According to Mieggue (1962), the promoters of the cult of Mary think that through the veneration of the Mother faith in the Son Jesus can be revived. This perspective helps to understand about this persistent devotion to the Saint; in a way she is remembered in the names given to women: *Mary, Mary of Aparecida, Conception of Aparecida;* on the other hand, she is seen in interjections, such as *the Virgin Mary, Our Lady,* Our, *Virgin!* and others. And in view of this, she is well remembered in the texts that have some Marian sense.

Given the great importance of Mary in Christian culture, this study makes reflections using the information contained in the chants. The development of concepts found in the texts happens gradually. They talk from the virginal pregnancy of Mary to his influence and follow up on the manifestations of her son Jesus.

---

1   The songs that are part of the collections published by the Catholic Church undergo a selection, so each diocese is responsible for organizing and spreading the hymns. I gathered the songs using books and websites that contained Marian hymns thus I looked for texts that explored the liberating idea of Mary and that had epithets and/or terms that qualified Mary.
2   Of the authors mentioned, it was discovered that only three are foreign, but remained in Brazil for some time.

Dogmas are also very imminent in the texts: The Divine Maternity of Mary, Virginity, the Immaculate Conception and Assumption. As eschatological symbols, these dogmas give a strong impetus to the compassionate and fair way of life[3] observed in the Marian songs, as well as indicating a definite perception of the holiness of Mary.

Therefore, there is a productive material, with epithets and adjectives treatments that are mainly entrusted to Mary. It is noticed that many of the titles are basically linked to the representation of "liberating Maria", there is also a significant amount of epithets that have relation to earthly life, biblical passages and Marian theology. Consequently, it was decided to separate the epithets as follows: theological, dogmatic, nationalist, popular, symbolic and family.

The classification of such epithets is essential in this work because it values the Marian text. Each title offers a purpose and this makes the songs have relevant purposes, with an idea of Mary to be moved and "accepted" by the devotees, who, through Marian songs end up getting religious experiences increasingly turned to Mary. And these experiences can also go back to the scientific community, which may expand the studies related to epithets present in many existing Marian songs.

The titles are the key elements of this research, as are present in the chants and part of their themes. These features make the Marian texts an important document that can be evaluated more thoroughly by opening avenues for studying the notion of epithets in hymns made to honor Mary.

---

3 See Coyle (1999).

1. THE RELIGIOSITY AND MARY

Picture: Mary carved in wood, sold at fairs and presented in local businesses. Image of the photograph belonging to Damiana Pinto "Dona Dazinha" - Ilha Solteira, São Paulo, Brazil.

When starting a discussion that evidences Mary, the mother of Jesus, it is important that we understand some of the Christian dogmas that help for a good understanding of the devotion to the saint.

Thus, the term *devotion* means sincere and fervent attachment to God or the saints, in a liturgical form or by regular private practices, where there is a religious feeling and infinite mercy:

> Devotion is still the queen of virtues, and the perfection of charity as the cream to the milk, the flower to the plant, the brightness for the precious stone and the scent to the balm, which exudes everywhere an odor of softness that comforts the spirit of the men and the angels rejoice. (SALES, 2002, p. 35).

This zeal is limited to the Catholicism universe - and, within it, in the religion, specifically the Popular Religiosity. *Devotion* terminology is popular and it acquired, throughout history, certain pejorative connotation by relativize the importance of the clerical hierarchy.

It was mainly developed in Christianity Colonial period[4], which in power maintenance issues, it had an interest in disqualifying the popular religious manifestations, thus maintaining control over the religious people. After the

II Vatican Council[5] there was a particular term replacement attempt *devotion* or *popular devotion to the* generic term *popular religiosity.*

---

4   Christianity "[...] it is a revival of a conception of the Church which lasted during the Middle Ages in Western Europe. The basic element of the model is the concept of sacral society. In this concept of sacral society or Christianity it is identified the concepts of faith and nationality, and the Catholicism becomes the official state religion. The interests of the Church are the interests of the state and vice versa [...] " (SCHLESINGER; PORTO, 1995, p 737.).

5   "The last Catholic Council (Vatican II, October 11, 1962 to December 8, 1965) was held under the sign of reconciliation and ecumenical unity. Convened by Pope John XXIII, with the participation of more than 2,000 bishops and superiors of religious orders, the Council attenuated the papal centralism, abolished the Latin liturgy, replacing it with local languages and it recognized the value of historical study methods of the religious subjects. " (ELIADE; COULIANO 1995: p. 120.).

This happened, as Pedro Oliveira (1988) says, since the beginning of the Romanization process of the Catholic Church, which is a process of religious reforms started over a hundred years in Europe, during the pontificate of Pius IX (1846-1878). It aimed to worldwide deploy a certain Catholicism standard, "the Roman model", which culminated in the Second Vatican Council, with the renewal of the liturgy, proposing among other changes, that the images of the saints lose place in the "sacred spaces" of the temples. This devotion was seen as something derogatory, faith demonstrations that did not fit the European mold.

The common language understood *devotion* as "the act to dedicate or consecrate to someone or to divinity [...]A religious sense, worship, religious practice, finally, an intimate dedication, an affection, affection for a special veneration object. " (DICTIONARY AURÉLIO, 2001, p. 233). Devotion is born, usually, from the belief in certain "supernatural" powers that the saint of devotion may have - often an extraordinary event, miracle or something that occurred or was heard it occurred in some situation.

In this sense, the scholar Azzi (1994) states that devotion to the saint is to the faithful guarantee of heavenly aid to its needs, and that loyalty to the holy manifests itself above all in the exact fulfillment of the promises made. Similarly, in the West, St. Augustine assigns, forcefully, a powerful impetus to this conception of faith-trust, prior to all religion and all intellectual elaboration of dogmatic content. In his short treatise on the *Utility of believe*, this says:

> If you should not believe what it is known, how, I wonder, the children submit to their parents and give them their affection if they not believe that they are their parents? By reason they can not know them, is the authority of the maternal testimony that makes to believe that such man is the father. And even on the mother, not her that ordinarily we refer, but the midwives, the wet nurses and domestic, since it may be that her child has been stolen and replaced by another and she herself, so deceived, mislead the others. However, we believe, and without hesitation, while recognizing that we can not know. Otherwise, do not see that family love, that sacred bond of humanity,

would be desecrated by a criminal pride? Who, then, even crazy, see as guilty a man who has been surrendered its son's duties to those who believe they are their parents, out of fear that can love in false? (SAINT AUGUSTINE[6] 1996 cited LE GOFF, 2006, p. 412).

However, a saint is not considered as such by chance, he is recognized for the acts at emanated love. There is a process that is being accepted in the community, even the types of requests that are diversified and that also assist in the expansion of devotional networks (BEINERT, 1979).

Accordingly, until the eleventh century, the canonization was given by uniformity of opinions; the proposals were sent to the Pope by the bishops, expressing the desire of the communities involved. The saint was basically

chosen by the people, however, the oral tradition was predominant and therefore it would contribute to the development of visionary stories (AUGRAS, 2005).

Many of these stories propagated by the people helped to promote some saints, the case of Mary was not much different. That devotion, that over time was multiplying, is more than a love to the chosen holiness, is a bond that lasts a lifetime. The devotee had to have a deep connection with the subject worthy of devotion, living in accordance with Christian life and walking in trying to keep a contact of absolute intimacy with the essentially pure subject.

However, to maintain a devotion and follow a devout life according to Sales (2002)[7], it is necessary to also participate in the life and victories won by the saint, maintaining daily contact and care for one who is getting closer to the devotee's life. The Christian must create models far removed from their daily routine for reaffirming contact with the saint and strengthen his own faith.

---

6   SANTO AGOSTINHO. A Virgem Maria: Marian hundred texts with comments. Sao Paulo: Paulus, 1996.
7   S. Francis de Sales has the title of Doctor of the Church, is the owner and patron of the Salesian family.

DEVOTION AND MARY

One of the most highlighted points of the Catholic Church is, to first order, devotion to Mary, Mother of God, then the angels and the saints. The New Testament texts that discuss the Saint are sober, but dense; several of them explicitly express the eminence of Mary and justify the broad interest of the Church by the Saint. They are like the "seven jewels" that adorn the Nazarene.

The importance of developing an examination of the issue stems primarily from the fact that Mary is not, in the Church's experience any figure, is a "central" figure, although not the center, which is always Jesus Christ.

This important figure, considered hyperdulia[8], it is synonymous of protection for many devotees, for this and for other reasons that it can be seen throughout this research that the veneration of Mary is constant and its religious figure is very welcome in the Christian or not, since it is about a woman who, because of her historical, brings together "all" the qualities of a saint and miraculous person.

It is notable that many wait for help and seek in Mary protection that perhaps can "not" be found in other saints; the news of healing and achievements spread, and so people want to receive the grace that had once been disclosed by those who received it, promoting increasingly the author of wonders.

From the saints, it is believed that Mary was the chosen by the ones dedicating a portion of their lives to devotions for those in need of aid and relief. Thinking about as large number of people who have that approach with Mary, several chapels were erected in several places in order to spread more and more devotion in the Nazarene.

In this perspective, most small churches from the colonial period were built by the devotion of lay people, often in fulfillment of promises made.

---

8   It is the special religious worship that the Catholic religion reserves for the Virgin Mary, higher than the dulia (dedicated to saints and angels).

18

On many occasions the local community was organized to take care of the sacred building and maintaining the service; it did not need to be in a very large space, enough to be a small space, the image and the visitors began to happen (AZEVEDO, 2001).

Admittedly, for almost two thousand years, the cult of Mary remains alive, although it has lost momentum in some periods. Although manifest mismatch between popular faith and the orthodoxies of the Church, its worship never faded and is currently one of the most remarkable phenomena of the Catholic media (PELIKAN, 2000).

One of the supports of this reinvigoration is the apparitions[9] and messages. They are stories of men and women, in most cases, poor and simple, which would have communicated with the Virgin. In many cases, the "miracle" ones ensured that they saw her, while in others, ensured they have had internal locutions, talks with the Saint during a type of trance.

The Church hierarchy, dissatisfied with the spread of such stories, warns that "Christian piety made of Mary, the Mother of the Lord, more than cult object than meditation, more praise than study." (PELIKAN, 2000, p. 18).

This Saint is synonymous of praise and exaltation in the religious environment, especially in the space of Catholicism. Taking into account the following prophecy: " all generations will call me blessed" (Luke, 1:48), it is clear that Mary increasingly becomes alive in popular devotions, because it conveys the idea that with the rise of sin, God devised a special creature, "without weakness spot" to generate the one who would redeem mankind.

Similarly, the Song of Songs (4: 7) says of Mary, "You are altogether beautiful, my friend; there is no flaw in you." Still there is the following comparison: "As the lily among thorns, so is my friend among the young" (Song of Songs 2: 2).

---

9   An illustrative example and widely reported by the media was the appearance of the image of the Virgin "stamped" on the window of a house on the periphery of Ferraz de Vasconcelos (SP), in July 2002.

Also, it can be observed through Saint Ambrósio words[10]: "No wonder the mother begins the work of him who came to redeem the world, so she withdrew freely first the fruit of salvation. Through she is noticing the salvation of all" (NEVES, 1918). The Mother of God, for being considered immaculate by the Catholic Church, and representative of the Father on earth, is the choice of the Catholic people to be venerated.

Following this reasoning, it is noted that in the New Testament there was a growing interest in the person of Mary. Despite the total absence of the Virgin in the Pauline writings, Matthew, Luke, and the fourth Gospel offer greater relevance and put her on important theological contexts. So, Mary's dogmas did not arise only by historical vision.

This search for authenticity about the Virgin in the dogmas is because she is seen as the "most perfect case of Christianity," thanks to the maternal faith and her believer maternity (MASCIARELLI[11] 1993 apud AZEVEDO, 2001).

On this subject, Rahner (1989 p. 43) writes: "Mary is the most perfect representation of what a Christian is, because with access of her faith in the physical concreteness of her divine motherhood, she received the one who is the salvation of all, Jesus Christ, our Lord."

Mary, hailed as the "Full of Grace" by the angel Gabriel (Luke, 1:28)[12] is the virgin who became the mother of the Son of God, so the statement of a sentence as dogma is the highest qualification in theology.

Turning to the visibility of "Full of Grace" in Brazil, the Marian Movement is noticeable in several ways. The most visible are the festivals that take place in Aparecida do Norte Sanctuary and in Belem do Pará where it is celebrated

10   St. Ambrose is the symbol of the Church, resurgent after suffered years of hidden life and the Roman persecutions.St. Augustine was his continued listener, as he mentioned in his Confessions, and having been baptized by him.
11   MASCIARELLI, Michele Giulio.Maria "LA CREDENTE". In: CONVEGNI MARIANI. Maria nel Catechismo della Chiesa Cattolica. Rome: Center of Marian Culture, 1993. p. 21-56.
12   Catechism of the Catholic Church, n.490 (VATICAN, 2008).

Nossa Senhora do Círio de Nazaré[13]. In addition to these, numerous titles are attributed to the Virgin Mary: Our Lady of Nazareth, Our Lady of Lourdes, Our Lady of Fatima, Our Lady of Mount Carmel, Our Lady of Rocio Our Lady of Guadalupe, among others. Thus, it is clear that the human and motherhood trait of Mary is always emphasized in the titles[14], and also assigned to her

---

13   Celebrations held throughout the first fortnight of October.
14   Pelikan (2000) indicates, in all, 156 names of the Virgin.

Figure: Aparecida Pantanal. Exhibition - Library of the Federal University of Grande Dourados, UFGD, on April 5, 2015.

DEVOTEES

Devotion to Mary greatly influences the collective or public processes of a society, either by a visibly political or military nature or by direct relation to the formation of national and social identity, including the question of charity, benevolence and mutual aid.

This Marian charity is a powerful mediation in that the religiosity of the people can be made historical practice. From this perspective, first comes the inculturation of the faith[15], and then its social practice is displayed. Faith is directly linked to popular piety and this is associated with the social commitment of each one (BOFF, C., 2006).

On the above, Pope John Paul II declared that the cultural reality, marked by the living presence of the Mother of God, is a potential that must be tapped in all its virtues evangelizing forward to the future, to drive people from the hands of Mary to Christ.

These people that has a devotion to Mary believe they receive from her an infinite protection, seeing in the charitable and protective Saint one solution indicative to existing problems. The cultural relationship that Saint has with the people are focused on the realization of all kinds of protection and deliverance, that are received and craved actions by people[16].

From the evangelization of popular religiosity, in this case dominated by the Marian piety, the person should take inspiration for urgent commitment for justice. In this regard, Pope John Paul II, Homily n. 6, made the following speech:

---

15   According to toLe Goff and Schmitt (2006, p. 412), the idea of faith (fides in Latin, pistis in Greek) is an original creation of Christianity, because from the Gospels and the Epistles of Paul, it combines the idea of an intellectual or emotional acceptance of the truth of the Christian message with a voluntary act, sustained by divine inspiration, in confidence in who transmits this direct message (Jesus) or indirectly (the community of believers, the Church).
16   These people are those who believe in Mary, regardless of their religions.

> It is necessary and urgent that the same Christian and Marian faith
> boost for a wide action in favor of peace for those people who are
> suffering for so long. It is necessary to implement effective justice
> measures to overcome the widening gap between those living
> in opulence and those who lack the most indispensable things [...]
> (BOFF, C., 2006, p. 93). [17]

It is noticed that the quoted thought evolved, from a conception of the
poor, defined as objects of care of Church and State, to a conception of little
favored, seen as subjects of their own liberation.

In this sense, the devotees believe in the power given to Mary by God; the
Pope's words confirm what people have said about the Marian faith and its
consequences for the social environment. Messages addressed to the people
by Pope John Paul II had a strong relationship with the faith established with
the Virgin, through which the words were uttered, for the most part, to the
poor and needy people, peasants, women, children and victims of injustice in
general.

Thus, speaking to the poor peasants of Colombia, the Pope presents, first,
the popular figure of Mary as Evangelization force, as seen in Homily n. 9:
"Mary ... approaches all, especially the poor, the most sublime mysteries of
our religion." (BOFF, C., 2006, p. 95). A message left by the top leader of the
Catholic Church progressively changes from a more passive gaze of the poor
for a more active stance, the latter being formed by beings who should be
released, making them timely redeeming people:

> Yourself thirsty, dear peasants, through your faith in God and your
> sense of honor, through your work and supported by adequate forms
> of association, able to defend your rights, the indefatigable builders
> of integral development, which bring seal of your humanity and your
> Christian conception of life ...The faith that the poor put on Christ
> and the hope they place in his kingdom have as a model and protector
> the Virgin Mary.[18] (BOFF, C., 2006, p. 95).

17   This same thought, according to the same logic of articulation, appears on the
papal message given at the time of the Angelus on December 13, 1987, the day after the feast
of Our Lady of Guadalupe (BOFF, C., 2006).
18   Homily number 9, of John Paul II.

On this fervent vision, the poor, following the model of the Virgin Mary, always seek to be near her and even closer to God, in junction with the search for solutions to the vicissitudes faced daily. The faith that some people have in the Virgen makes the approach to the Saint to be found in many different environments. The history of Marian piety witness, like all living reality, that the Virgin was growing spiritually through the ages, from the experience and proximity to others. This story carries the prophecy of the same Mary: "Henceforth all generations will call me blessed" (Luke, 1:48). Generations, even after some declines suffered by the Catholic Church continue to believe in the liberating power of Mary.

2. MARY IN LATIN AMERICA

In the immense lands that surround our planet, there are independent ways of worshiping a saint. In Latin America, a devastated and slaved place by explorers, there is a particular way a trace of religious people's dependence on the worship of the Virgin. The story of those who most need support, food, health, education, etc., is still present and known for groups that keep the faith and come from the simplicity and persecution - and it is based not only on official documents deemed worthy of being preserved, but on the conventional wisdom in the transmitted traditions, in the religious symbolism.

The scholar Hoonaert (1979) comments on this subject.

> There is no other way to know the history of Jesus of Nazareth, the chosen people, the apostles, martyrs, saints, the Christian fervor through the ages. The religious symbolism, for example, is a valid source for research of people's life, because their lineage is sincere, although it's difficult to interpret. (HOONAERT, 1979, p. 13).

Based on the above quoted passage, it is possible to consider that Mary is the symbolic archetype and the chosen evangelization in Latin America; one that was always next to Jesus, often in moments of pain and suffering, with which the oppressed people feel identified. In history, she marked in people the prospect of hope, liberation with the cross and death (painful virgin), identification with the people's problems (Cana), availability (visit to Elizabeth) and now she is remembered by many political and economic refugees (escaping into Egypt), missing and martyred (the cross, loneliness) for her strength, hope, victory and missionary presence (MARINS, 1986).

Thus, the devotees who identify with Mary, taking into account those from Latin America that make sacrifices at times of distress and difficulty, have a dedication to the Holy that in a way represents her people and culture: Our Lady of Aparecida , of Penha, of Guidance, of Grace; of Exile, indicating nostalgic for the homeland; Our Lady of Wonders (charm); of Liberation, of the Refuge, of Good Success and of Piety (gratitude); and representations of

Our Lady of Sorrows, of Conception and of the Rosary reflect the experiences in the mills (Azevedo, 2001).

This predominance of Marian devotion comes from the maternal and protector role given to Mary at the beginning of the colonization of Latin America (century. XVI); the Virgin is considered the symbol of the Church from the earliest times of Christianity.

For the most part, all of Latin American countries and much of their population turn to Mary using the various known qualifying treatments. The Virgin is the patroness of several Latin American countries. Her images are rich in detail, bringing in many situations traces of her people.

In those countries, there is a very characteristic Marian devotion, starting with Mexico where the apparition of the Virgin of Guadalupe is the first record of this devotion. We can present other important shrines dedicated to Mary, Our Lady of Luján (Patroness of Argentina); Our Lady of Copacabana (Patroness of Bolivia); Our Lady of Mount Carmel, patroness of Chile (of the Chilean Army); Our Lady of Chinquinquirá, patron saint of Colombia (it was taken to the battlefield in the struggle for independence from Colombia, on the victory day it received the sword of Símon Bolívar as a gift); Our Lady of Charity (patron saint of Cuba); Our Lady of Quinche (patron saint of Ecuador); Our Lady of Suyapa (patroness of Honduras); Our Lady La Purisima (patron saint of Nicaragua); Our Lady of the Thirty-Three (patron saint of Uruguay); Our Lady of Coromoto (patron saint of Venezuela); Our Lady of Caacupé (Paraguay patron); and Our Lady of Aparecida (patron saint of Brazil) (BOFF, C., 2006; MARCELO, 2006).

In this scenario, it appears that Latin America is a quite expansive Marian devotion. The religious acts connected to Mary outweigh the differences of languages and territorial boundaries established through a "by force" process

of colonization and domination. So even after five hundred years, this religiosity remains firm and consolidated in many different social settings.

The intercessions for Mary were constant by the faithful catholic in Latin America and it continues nowadays, even with several changes in the religious core, taking as an example the statement of the evangelical churches, which often preach one feeling more profane about the image of Our Lady of Aparecida chosen as patroness of Brazil and several other locations.

OUR LADY OF APARECIDA, THE PATRON SAINT OF BRAZIL

The analysis of the facts does not happen differently in Brazil, which was dominated by the colonizers for centuries, and even today it fights against problems that should have come out of the list of issues. These are still unresolved: racism, health, hunger, religious intolerance, among others.

The people in need of religious support, eager for healing, forgiveness, deliverance and other desires, seek in Mary of Nazareth a motherly support. The Virgin plays the role of the "Great Mother", that one that protects from all dangers. For this archetype and other social functions, Mary occupies a unique place in the hearts of the vast majority of the Brazilian catholic people, being venerated in all the virtues and privileges as Mother of God, intercessory and universal mediator.

Only the theological greatness of Mary can't be a reason enough to explain their socio-historical merit, it must add the anthropological dimension, in which the Virgin became a model of a society and the pattern of searches and dreams of a people in the social history. So, if Mary of Nazareth as a person has developed in the famous character of Our Lady of Aparecida, it was because of the feelings and experiences that inhabit the religious soul of a people.

This representation of Mary is very present also in missionary souls of priests and religious, who sailed for months by the seas in search of new land. They presented God, one and three, through the Virgin Mary and then built several patron saints, which had the mission to mediate access to the Christ to the divine protection (Azevedo, 2001).

Even with the various chapels set in places where foreign conquerors transited, in the Brazilian case, Mary's figure was only publicly recognized since the finding of the statue of Our Lady, in 1717, in the village of Guaratingueta, São Paulo, when it was "initiated" in fact the Marian devotion.

It was through three fishermen that the image of Mary was found, they were working in the Paraiba River in order to bring fish to be served to a distinguished visitor of the village, the Governor D. Pedro de Almeida, Assumar Count, representative of the Portuguese court.

Just the fact that the Saint's image has been found was considered the first miracle, considering that in that river, too bulky, it was virtually impossible to find objects heavier than water that were not set out in the watercourse background. The second miracle was the large number of fish caught after the discovery of the image of the Mother of God (Azevedo, 2001).

This abundant fishery may be considered a prodigious miracle, similar miracle to what the New Testament describes that occurred in the waters of the Sea of Tiberias (Lake of Gennesaret) in Galilee. In this passage, Jesus risen, to be known to the Apostles, sent to cast the net on the right side the boat. And he said unto them to cast the net on the right side of the ship and ye shall find. They cast therefore, and now they were not able to draw it for the multitude of fishes. (John 21: 1-14).

The good news of prodigious act occurred in the village spread very quickly, bringing from there a fervent devotion to Mary. The unrivaled fervor to the Holy materialized on the individual level, the sacrifices, the prayers, the offers made on her behalf, at the collective plan and at parties in her honor (MACHADO, 1969).

Since the beginning, the presence of Mary gave dignity to the enslaved ones, hope for the exploited ones and motivation for the liberation movements so it could not deny the devotion to the Saint. In this way, devotion of praise and honor to the Mother of God have been developed over the years in Brazil.

Thus, the expansion of Marian devotion in Brazil walked along with the State of São Paulo in the development process: most of the time, people who were passing through the way Rio-São Paulo, stopped to visit churches that held the statue of the Virgin. As an example of such visits, it is essential to mention the visit made by Princess Isabel, on 6 November 1884, which pointed out in her paper that she stopped in Guaratinguetá "to climb to the chapel of Our Lady of Aparecida and to pray. " (Augras, 2005, p. 36).

The accommodation for the image of the Saint had to receive repairs over the years, because the hits from the time when the image was found increased. Large altars were built and the representation of Our Lady of Aparecida now has more and more notoriety of the devotees throughout Brazil, which honored, and still honor fervently.

However, only at the end of the 20th century, in 1900, the first official pilgrimages were organized in Brazil, representing the Catholic population of São Paulo and Rio de Janeiro. And in 1904, the São Paulo episcopate obtained from Pope Pius X the solemn coronation of the statue of the Saint.

After thirty years of entire dedication of the devotees to Mary, the need was felt to acclaim the image of the Holy further, titled "Brazilian Saint". For this purpose, the bishops of Brazil asked the Pope Pius XI that the representation of Our Lady of Aparecida was publicly granted as the patroness of Brazil.

Thus, the statue of Our Lady of Aparecida was transported by train to the Federal Capital, where Sebastian Leme formalized the patronage ceremony in the presence of Getulio Vargas, who at that moment of the devotees' joy, kissed the feet of the symbolic image of Mary (SOUZA, 1996).

Even before these events, Father José Alves Vilela had succeeded in 1745 in Rome, the license to the official cult of plastic representation of Mary and to build a chapel. For this, he presented three miracles attributed to the Saint: candles that were lit without explanation, the occurrence of tremors in the altar niche and hearing noises from the chest where the image was. "It is possible that without the work of Father Vilela, the cult around the image had not reached the projection we know nowadays" says the researcher Martha dos Reis (1999). He took for himself a domestic religious expression and developed it in a region full of conflicts and sufferings, in which the attachment to the faith can be seen as a natural consequence of life's pains.

After events such as those cited above, there was a strong race of the devout society of the time to meet the statue of Our Lady of Aparecida. Everything happens as if in the theological content of the mystery of Mary, there was a destination already carved that would make her what she became in the course of the history of Marian devotion in Brazil.

IS VIRGIN MARY A MYTH?

For many people the figure of Mary is a myth, leading to think of the phenomenon of her popularity in two directions: the individual and her need for communion with the sacred and for the social existence as represented.

In either case, Mary is established as a symbol and as such is surrounded by theories. So as the perceptual state that involves a certain look of the world in the case related to faith, as the symbolic imaginary translator of identities and aspirations.

Regarding the devotees of Mary, it could be understood that to contemplate her in her holiness, they share this sanctification, which means that two moves are made: the first occurs when they get closer to this sacred condition of the symbol, and the second is when they move away from the profane state that their worldviews consider inappropriate.

This idea of the existence of an aggressive world means that there is an understanding in changing the behavior of people, since this is directly linked to the interpretation that they make about reality. It also can be noted that this impression of the world judges a reality and not the reality itself, hence the fact that it is different for everyone. Every human perceives an object or a situation according to the aspects that are important to themselves.

However, the object perceived needs to have basis of a person in reality, because otherwise, it may literally not perceive it. Mary is perceived as holy and Mother of God, because her story can confirm it many times. The church and the gospel seek to reveal the importance of Mary for humanity.

The understanding and perception of the existence of the figure of Mary are focused on the satisfaction, pleasure, finally for reasons and mainly to emotions and feelings that move the way that every person is, especially the interest, necessity and expectation to achieve the expected help.

The perception is evaluated as part of the process of knowledge and depending on what is observed, the visual component becomes essential, because the notion of space is processed from the physical form, which is decisively perceived by sight.

As far as the religious community is dedicated to Mary, who is considered the "chosen of the Lord," is symbolically placed in the ranks of the chosen one and getting out, even in the abstract way, from the body of the excluded.

When relating the visual perception of faith devotees dedicate to the Virgin Mary, so it is referred to the space physically constructed, the world as it exists, as the position that the person, in this case the devotee, holds within this world in a process resizing of being / to be in life.

In this sense, Christianity, which takes Jesus Christ as its founder starts to expand geographically throughout the Earth and it is the largest example of such expansion; which was supported by the action of the Roman Empire (until the fourth century) and virtually occupying the entire universe known that time - the expansion continues to the present. With the discoveries of the 16th century, the trade facilitated the Christian expansion. To the Christian expansion in Roman times to the present there are sacred places ranging in size and importance, like a small crucifix by the roadside to large sanctuaries such as the Basilica of Our Lady of Aparecida, in the State of São Paulo (FRANCE 1972).

However, the approach taken here brings into focus more than in a geographical point. The need to highlight concerns in the sacralization of the world and the insertion of the religious man in this space, that from the way it is perceived, established other kind of relationships between man himself and the world, based on the sacred worship.

This sanctification of the world-space corresponds to the attempt to guidance for goals that are beyond the limitations and secular bias. Despite this profane condition appears predominantly at present, the opposition between sacred and profane, that as a rule guides the vision that defines spheres of human life, shows up dead when it considered that,

> whatever the degree of desacralization of the world to which it has arrived, the man who chose a profane life can not completely abolish religious behavior [...] even the existence of more desacralized still retains traces of a religious valorization of the world. (ELIADE, 1983, p. 37).

The existence marked by the sacred is that one taken in its entirety, away from the relativity which marks the profane sphere of life.

> [...] The sacred is the real par excellence, at the same time is the power, efficiency, source of life and fertility. The desire of the religious man of living in the holy, amounts in fact to his desire of being in objective reality, to not let himself to paralyze by endless relativity of purely subjective experiences and of living in a real and efficient world - not an illusion. (ELIADE, 1983, p. 42).

Each and every understanding that can articulate on the religious experience leads us to think about what is lived. That is, the understanding of man's relationship with the sacred presupposes to understand all levels of experience depth of the religious phenomenon.

From the point of view of religion, faith would be a lift design, identity and communion with significant representations not only of the supreme, but of perfection, or closer of what is called human way, of a fullness always desired but never achieved by way of the profane aspects that curtail the experience of life.

This experience of the religious phenomenon imposes the attempt to understand the unknown elements in certain societies considered less valued. The popularity of sacred symbols, in this case, of the Virgin Mary, shows the religiosity differently but at the same time generating meaning to society. Thus religious phenomena are not only accidental or a result of social expectations, but also encouragement, even partly, their own social structures.

Regardless of historical feature that Christianity assumes in the Western world, and particularly in Latin America, where it served as a substrate for the colonization process, including therein missions not even close to be sacred as the decimation of native peoples and the enslavement of black people. The phenomenon of Marian devotion resizes social meanings to the proportion that are placed in contrast to the social conditions of existence.

In this context, it is important to emphasize that the figure of Mary has its greatest support in the lower classes, which gives the issue the aspect of popular religiosity, with its peculiarities, among which stands out the ambiguity between acceptance of the sacred as opposed to the profane inside this. It is therefore the mercantilist context that takes place in processions, especially in the Basilica of Our Lady of Aparecida, Patroness of Brazil.

In these terms, the perception symbol of Mary as holy icon is also of overcoming, because

> [...] Beings and cultural objects are never given, they are put by certain social and historical practices, by forms of sociability of the inter-subjective and group relationships, of class, of the relationship with the visible and the invisible, with the time and space, with the possible and the impossible, with the necessary and the contingent. (CHAUÍ, 1989, p. 122).

Individually, each life means a willingness to exist, a need to be, a realization of favorable and unfavorable experiences. If in front of a religious phenomenon it must conclude the presence, the categorization and the values of an invisible world. In contrast, it is because the visibility attaches importance to addiction and the need to pursue any existing thing in our individualities, through the construction of mental and imaginary buildings.

As there are several ways to see the world, each image and idea about it are located from personal experience, learning and memory. All kinds of experiences, from the most linked to the daily life of the human being to the most distant from the everyday world, make up the individual framework of reality.

It is further considered that human perception can present another factor range, a hallucinatory element that alters the perception of an individual, as in the case of affective and magical but for the other principle of rationality. In this case,

> [...] It is not only the intrusion of an emotional or magical component that can fool us in our perceptions, it is also a running of a component seemingly logical and rational. In other words, we should be suspicious of our perception, not only of what seems absurd, but also of what seems obvious because it is logical and rational. (MORIN, 1986, p. 25).

Since perception is not only a reflection of what is noticed, what happens in this complex process flows in coding and translation of stimuli, which will lead to a representation of what is perceived by structuring it and organizing it to produce the real.

Therefore, it is important to understand that image, imagination and imaginary etymologically come from the same Latin root, *imago-ginis*, and have similar meanings such as symbolic figuration of an object or a mental reproduction of a sensation in the absence of the cause that produced it. That is developed from experiences, memories and perceptions, which reproduce the figure, in this case, the image of Mary.

The *Imaginarium*, in turn, is the key word and corresponds to the imagination as its function and product. The compound of mental images is defined from many different perspectives, even conflicting, as it is sometimes regarded as essentially open and evasive, sometimes it appears as the experience of opening and novelty. One way or another, the imaginary is located in the field of representation, but as a non-breeding translation, but creative and poetic, because, as much as part of the representation, in its intellectual aspect, the imagination surpasses it (DURAND , 1997).

Thus, Mary is not a fanciful fable, she is a living reality which the religious use as a practical and transcendent way at the same time. Marian symbolic expression covers aspects of both, the immediate life and the targeted destinations, but only the ones expected by faith that the preciousness that comes, meets the moral aspirations, so human.

The Durand researcher (1997, p. 14) says that the imagination is the "set of images and relationships of images, the thought capital of *homo sapiens*"; therefore, it grounds and calls the procedures of human thought. The imaginary dynamism by giving it a reality and essence, shows that, at least in principle, the logical thinking is not separated from the image. This would be the messenger of a captive sense of imaginary meaning, a figurative sense, being a motivated sign, so that means a symbol.

The order of this representation corresponds to a repertory of revealing man's life, in a dynamic way and it's not uncommon to be conflicting. In a relation between symbol and imaginary there are tension and shock camps, which lead us to consider that, depending on the perspective to be considered,

> The classification of the great symbols of the imagination in different motivating categories presents with effect great difficulties, because of the fact of non-linearity and the semantic content of the images; if it begins of well-defined objects through the frames of logic tools, as do the classic 'keys of dreams', it falls rapidly by the massiveness of the motivations, in an inextricable confusion. (DURAND, 1997, p. 33).

Not without reason, the multiplication of aspects that the symbol acquires, the thinker warns that his juxtaposition to visions merely Cartesian or "merely" structural and socially structured may constitute a fallacy. For the author, these explanations:

> [...] Cannot realize this fundamental power of symbols which is to connect, beyond the natural contradictions, the irreconcilable elements, social partitioning and segregation of periods of history. It becomes, then, necessary to seek the motivating categories of symbols on the basic behaviors of the human psyche, allowing for later the adjustment of such conduct to the directs complement or even the semiotic games. (DURAND, 1997, p. 38).

Thus, it can understand the symbolism is linked to a visual significance, since its structure is at the root of any thought. In the context of individuality, or its social character, the imagination arising from the subjective combined to the influences of social, returns in the form of product creation, testifying imaginary reality and social objectivity.

The strength of the relationship - reality/imagination - occurs due to the significant process, which acts as a true catalyst of this double position as emphasized Durand (1997), "the imaginary not only manifested itself as an activity that changes the world, as creative imagination, but above all as euphemistically transformation of the world, as *intellectus sanctus*, as the ordinance to be better orders. " (P.432)

Thus the religious man, when symbolizes the imaginary, establishes a close relationship between representation and the represented object and when doing so, it begins to manifest his identity:

> [...] Imagination and reality are also related, as much as possible to create an artwork, an object or a tool that does not correspond to any real object. So the experience - expanded by imagination - is embodied in a product. (KRAMER, 1993, p. 78).

The symbolic can be seen as the record of human activities in relation to real, in part unconscious, partly conscious and connected to the rules of representation, and the function of the signifier and the laws of culture.

Thus, the symbols, especially religious, are the first and original reading of the world. And when the man saturates the weakness of rational explanations, which do not subsidize a better understanding of life, it comes back to shelter in faith, to be reborn in the modern world, despite its ambiguities, it makes its experience to have a possible compatibility between sacred and profane.

In the case of Marian songs, these are products (at the same time provocative) both in a focused insight into the sacred as a willing imagination of a close future maybe different from the socioeconomic, cultural and historical conditions settings.

The fact is that as language exercise, the chants witness more than a religious phenomenon, they defend a world view motivated by faith in something different and consecrated by laws that differ from the standards present in the secular sphere.

To this question of religious experience, the experimentation of the sacred indicates that its various manifestations, whether individual or collective, as noted by Emile Durkheim (1998), appear in the states of social unrest when the sacred time stops the profane time of social and economic activities.

Etymologically, the term *sacred* (sacrum) comes from the Latin *sacer*, which comes in turn from *sancire*: to make something come true, check validity. The term *sancire* was affixed to the laws, to the institutions, to a state of things, to a fact. Thus, the etymology of the word clearly indicates the true and valid existence of the sacred as a way at the same time complementary and essential to human life (LE GOFF; SCHMITT, 2006).

In these terms, among the sacred symbols that modernity involves, Marian cults have been made in mobilizing religious devotion. To this view, Mary is the great symbol of support of the Catholic faith, as much as codes of conduct and as the religious female managers.

Marian apparitions motivate great praise of pilgrims who crave renewal in the life, in the construction of new meanings. They could also reaffirmed the Catholic faith to the "Blessed Virgin", and some people even return to the Catholic religion through these worship service.

The Marian "myth" breaks the alleged hegemony of the secular dimension and makes eminent the sacred vision of different images, the different senses of Mother, highlighting the image of the protection of the "Great Mother" in emotional consolations scenes, the revival of feelings, the construction of cultural choices and the impasses in existential dilemmas.

The constitution of Marian religiosity points out to a relationship of familiarity with the imaginary of motherhood and for the feminine dimension in the meanings of images of Mary - archetype of Mother, Woman and Divinity.

3. THE EPITHETS IN MARIAN SONGS

This chapter provides an analysis of some Marian songs, highlighting those found epithets. It is the main aspect of this book, its content shows an approach to these hymns sometimes poorly explored in the academic sphere, but very present in the popular media.

These compositions are present in many song books in most of Catholic churches in Brazil, being found today in places whose purpose is the dissemination of texts that mention Mary. Latin America, Central America and North America also have similar aspects of the Mother of God in their songs, each region present titles in their own ways, customs and traditions.

These songs in question have not undergone linguistic changes. Reliable copies of the Marian hymns were made for this study, to mention to the one who plays the role of "mother" of the Catholic Church and the poor people. Many composers, from the earliest centuries, make hymns in honor of the saint, troubadours like Alfonso X (century XIII), author of the Songs of the Holy Mary, classical artists, musicians, priests, enslaved people and others left immortalized numerous compositions honoring the one who once said: "For behold, from this time on all generations will count me blessed." (Luke, 1:48).

In contemporary times, a wide collection of music with popular rhythms can be expected to always recall the figure of Mary. Many religious and Marian devotees, in the case of Brazil, already sung or heard of "Mary of Nazareth" of the Father Zezinho and many other chants. The processions or Marian pilgrimages, the rosaries, litanies, are elements that together with the hymns are part of the texts made in honor of "Mother of God". Thus, the songs selected to be part of this book show mainly varied epithets, which are the key elements for this study and provide a lot of information related to the history of devotion to Mary.

Thereby, the figure of the Mother of God is manifested in Catholic religious songs because it is believed that these are the way of closeness and identification with the man. The hymns in question are those endowed with more expression, which made references to the image of Mary and were chosen with the intention of identifying the quality terms and epithets that exist in these chants, the main elements of this study.

Through the own titles of the songs it could be found the terms of qualifying and assignment treatments directed to the Mother of God. The texts are quite objective when they are dealing with elements that adorn the chants made in honor of Mary.

Knowing that Mary was the center in Christianity and still is today, it is quite common for hymns and beautiful poems to be written in tribute to her, which take into account the different terms used to refer to the Mother of God. In this sense, the researcher Clodovis Boff (2006) says that such terms and considerations to the Saint are clearly remembered, because it is basically a central figure, after Jesus, in Christianity:

> Her titles of excellence from the standpoint of faith are well known: **the mother of God, Holy Mary, Cause of our joy, blessed among women, that one that all generations will call her blessed** and also **the immaculate, the gloriously assumed into heaven, Queen, etc**.(BOFF, C., 2006, p. 287, emphasis added).

These qualifying treatments given to the Saint are very common and it is still possible to find various titles in the poems and songs that surround the Christian setting or not, at different times of our time, always emphasizing the importance of Mary figure in the religious environment.

Based on the titles present in the songs, it's very important to stress that because of devotion to Mary and their religious manifestations being extensive, it was decided to develop the study of epithets found from the Marian dogma: Mary is the Mother of God; she remained a virgin (Virgin Mary); it was conceived without sin (Immaculate Conception) and finally, after her sojourn on earth, she was taken up in body and soul into heavenly glory (Assumption of the Virgin Mary) (SILVA, 1994).

Thus, taking into account the above dogmas, it is started here the analysis of the song "Queen of the Assumption" that immediately makes us notice a title of nobility, an expression of "divine kingship" that Mary conveys.

The poem identifies the special mission given by God to Mary, who had the necessary quality to perform the task assigned by God. Only with one word, Mary, with her "let it be", enters the copious stream of poor people chosen by God, those ones who almost don't wonder, question or protest, but leave quietly and put their trust in the powerful hands of God. The boundary line drawn for this special mission consists primarily on simplicity and faith of the Holy (LARRAÑGA, 1980).

Through the ideas of the author's chants[19] there is a "special mission" of Mary, who according to Christian teaching was the one that gave birth to Jesus Christ:

Mary conceived without original sin, brought the light of life on Christmas Eve! You were immaculate in your conception, Oh predestined mother of the new creation. [...]	Maria concebida sem culpa original, trouxeste a luz da vida na noite de Natal! Tu foste imaculada na tua conceição, ó mãe predestinada da nova criação. [...]

For these reasons, Mary gave birth to Christ still being a virgin and had no sins. It was precisely because she is a pure woman and devoid of sins, chosen among many to give birth to "Our Saviour", on Christmas Eve.

Without making mistakes since her birth, Mary is coated with different meanings and completed, since her "destiny" was to be the mother of the life, the great matrix of life, she represents the possibility of generating the

eternal life, being a "damp earth" that participating in the offspring of God, represents the nativity image, becoming part of human tissue. The Virgin herself becomes the "Divine Mother" of beings:

19   *Song Rainha da Assunção.* (Queen of the Assumption)

| Mary of the Assumption, hear our voice, and call for protection to each of us. [...] | Maria da Assunção, escuta a nossa voz, e pede proteção a cada um de nós. [...] |

Here, the composer describes the Saint as "Mary of the Assumption", which refers to the rise of Her body into heaven, when she again met her soul[20]. It is the fourth dogma concerning the life of the Virgin Mary, whose proclamation took place in the mid-twentieth century. As did Pius IX for the dogma of the Immaculate Conception; in 1946, Pius XII also sent a letter to the world's bishops to hear their views on the infallible definition advisability of the bodily Assumption of Mary into heaven.

The agreement of the ecclesiastical base is recorded in the inscription that can be read on the inner wall of the central portico of St. Peter's Basilica,

> With the expectation of the Catholic world and with insistent votes, it was brought the 1st November of the Holy Year of 1950, when Pius XII in front of the fervency crowd that filled the St. Peter's Square, declared with infallible oracle that the Virgin Mary Mother of God was assumed body and soul into heaven. (BOFF, C., 2006, p. 523).

The dogma holds that Mary, after his death, ascended bodily into heaven as Christ after the Resurrection. Some ancient traditions say that she is not dead, just asleep, so it also exists the "Dormition of Mary" expression.

This Mary compound the preludes of the lordship of Christ over death. She is considered the human concrete reality perfectly glorified, the first link of land that connects the anchor thrown beyond the veil, "We have this hope as a sure and steadfast anchor of the soul, which enters the Inner Place behind the veil" (Hebrews 6:19).

The own Easter of the people is confirmed by Mary. In this view, it is raised the principle of resurrection, but the Ascendant in body and soul into heaven,

---

20   Cf. dogma defined by Pope Pius XII on November 1st 1959.

becomes through divine promise, to further ensure the return of the people to life. Like her, the faithful can scream harder, "Death has been swallowed up in victory" (1 Corinthians, 15:54). Thus, it can be understood that death suffered two sequential defeats: The Resurrection of Christ and then and because of this, the Assumption of Mary.

Such as maternity of the Holy ensures the incarnation of Jesus in history, so is the rise of the body of Mary into heaven that guarantees the resurrection of the body of Jesus and the redemption of our body (BOFF, C., 2006)[21].

In Brazil, the image of the Saint chosen as the representative of that which rose to heaven is, since colonial times, revered by the name of *Our Lady of the Good Death*, influenced the emergence of several brotherhoods[22], like the one in the city of Cachoeira, Bahia, and Carmo Convent in Olinda. The Assumption of Mary into Heaven had also originated the *Our Lady of Glory*, celebrated on August 15 and much known among devotees (Augras, 2005).

She is the "eternal sign of love"; if Jesus represents the love of God, Mary is the story of love in her various inventions, fantasies and divine madness. Moreover, this corresponds to the uniqueness of Marian epistemology, that in the act of God in Mary, does not only seek the necessary, but it also wants to respond to the convenient (BOFF, C., 2006).

The Holy is called like that because she gave birth to the Savior. After generating the child lit and after having accompanied the life of Jesus until his death, she was raised to heaven by angels sent by God. As a bright light, the Holy, according to the following excerpt, was exalted by the Lord.

---

21   In Latin: *Quod diuturnis catholicus orbis expectabat votis calendae novembris anni sacri MCML tulere cum in petriano forum ovantium multitudine referto ...Pius XII ... deiparam Virgninem Mariam anima et corpore in coelum assumptam falli nescio pronuntiabat oráculo [...]*(BOFF, C., 2006, p. 521).
22   Brotherhood, kinship bond between brothers, affectionate and intimate friendship between different people; fellowship, association, religious grope (HOUAISS, 2001).

Mary, dear mother, eternal sign of love! In the womb you gave life and body to the Savior! To the heaven You were raised by angels of the Lord, in the crowning glory, covered in splendor. [...]	Maria, mãe querida, sinal do eterno amor! No ventre deste a vida e corpo ao Salvador! Ao céu foste elevada por anjos do Senhor, na glória coroada, coberta de esplendor. [...]

After being assumed into heaven, the woman of Nazareth, covered by the divine light, obtained the power to protect, with her veil, the people who walked into the light. She mediates between earth and heaven, following the souls of the dead to go into the sky. She serves the role of that one who holds the key to heaven and makes good use of the powers given by the Lord.

Mary, Queen mother protect with your veil, the people who walks toward the sky. You were the wonder of the works of the Lord, wife, mother and daughter of the same God of love [23].	Maria, mãe rainha protege com teu véu, o povo que caminha na direção do céu. Tu foste a maravilha das obras do Senhor, esposa, mãe e filha do mesmo Deus de amor

Mary, Mother of God, called the "Wonder of the works of the Lord," the highest degree of excellence, is recognized as *wife, mother and daughter* of the God of love. High to heaven, the Virgin owns the three feminine nouns above.

Leonardo Boff (1990) says that the Virgin as wife first emerges as a bride, promise of life and collected source, whose waters have not been channeled. After the maternal intimacy, there is the spousal, which is the most fulfilling of human experiences. Being wife-bride near and distant at the same time.

---

23   Song Rainha da Assunção (Queen of the Assumption in English)

She is close by love and confident communion; by the charm she has on her lover. She is far, because it still remains a promise, not fully realized offering; everything on the wife-bride is about to blossom and bear fruit. It is in this interrelationship that the value of Mary's virginity shines, and represents the archetype of the whole, closed in on itself but open for playback.

Also according to the theologian Leonardo Boff (1990), it appears that the Saint, as a mother, is linked to the mystery of life; this means she was the first continent that the child discovers. It is through the mother figure that the child psychologically prepares the preliminary guidelines of existence in terms of good and evil, acceptance or rejection.

And as a daughter of God, Mary is "blessed among women", an expression that reflects a Semitism expressing the superlative: "the most blessed among women." In her lifetime, it was unveiled to the high calling: the called women compared to men and in relation to God. She reveals the radical dimension of human, women's, and thus it is made exemplary not only for women but for all human beings, becoming as a wife and daughter, a new facet of the superior deity.

VIRGIN OF THE ROSARY

The song in question begins with the qualifying word "Virgin of the Rosary", and some of the main events related to the annunciation, conception and assumption of Mary will be highlighted, since the hymn makes room for the expansion to study these elements.

One of the most important characteristics of poetry in the existential reflection of Mary is shown in the chant. In this hymn, it also appears religiosity of an author who escapes from simple assessments and searches the idealization of the Virgin with a momentum of a romantic poet:

Virgin of the Rosary	Virgem do Rosário
You are a lovely rose	Sois rosa mimosa
Among the other flowers	Entre as outras flores
You are the most beautiful	Sois a mais formosa
[...]	[...][24]

Mary is equated with a rose, which exudes scents, whether mild, pleasant or sweet, she is seen here as an unparalleled rose. Also the genre of mimosas: mimosa rose is a plant that brings many species of herbs, shrubs, vines and trees together, native to tropical and subtropical regions, especially in Americas, some weed, several grown as ornamental, few as medicinal, for extraction of firewood (HOUAISS, 2001).

In the second stanza of the chant, there is the sense that serves as the starting point for devotees to praise the current memories of the mysteries that make mention of the wonders and sufferings of Mary:

Praise devotees,	Louvemos devotos,
The pious memories	As pias memorias
Of Rosary the joys	Do rosário os gozos
The pains and glories.	As dôres e glorias.
[...]	[...]

The Rosary of the Virgin Mary, *Rosarium Virginis Mariae*, was taken into shape gradually in the second millennium, it is a beloved prayer by many saints and encouraged by the Magisterium [25], the word rosary is linked to that prayer.

In its simplicity and depth remains, even when the third millennium just started, this is a prayer of great significance and intended to produce fruits of holiness. It fits perfectly in the spiritual path of a Christianity that after two

thousand years, has lost none of its original freshness and feels impelled by the Spirit of God to "put out into the deep" (*duc in altum!*) to reaffirm Christ as Lord and Savior, as "the way, the truth and the life" (John 14: 6).

---

24   Emphasis added.In the hymns which the interpretations are made, we will take the liberty to highlight them for the best understanding of the reader.
25   Concerning the last apostolic letter of Pope John Paul II - Rosarium Virginis Mariae, LG. number 58

There is also the epithet "Virgin of the Rosary" at the next entitled chant[26], the "Virgin of the Rosary":

Virgin of the Rosary,	Virgem do Rosário,
Odorant rose,	Odorante rosa,
Among all the flowers,	Entre as flôres tôdas,
You're the most beautiful!	És a mais formosa!
[...]	[...]

Mary is described as the most beautiful of all flowers, the author emphasizes that the Saint is a rose that gives off pleasant scents; however, distinguished from other "roses" that do not have this attribute.

Virgin of the Rosary,	Virgem do Rosário,
In Aparecida,	Em Aparecida,
Fatima or Lourdes,	Fátima ou Lourdes,
Be our sentry box!	Sê nossa guarida!
[...]	[...]

The "Virgin of the Rosary", according to this chant[27], is considered the guardian anywhere, whether in Aparecida (Aparecida do Norte / SP),there is one of the biggest Mary's sanctuaries in the world. Fatima or Lourdes are two places of worship equally visited.

Virgin of the Rosary,	Virgem do Rosário,
In life and in death,	Na vida e na morte,
Be your mysteries	Sejam teus mistérios
Our strong shield!	Nosso escudo forte!

The Rosary, in fact, even if characterized by its Marian physiognomy, at its core is a Christocentric prayer. In the sobriety of its elements, it focuses on the depth of the entire Gospel message which is almost a compendium. It echoes the prayer of Mary, her perennial *Magnificat* for the work of the redemptive incarnation which began in her virginal womb.

---

26   *Song Virgem do Rosário* (Virgin of the Rosary).
27   Ibid.

With it, the people attend the school of Mary to leave themselves to be introduced in the contemplation on the face of Christ beauty, and in the experience of his love's depth. Through the Rosary, the believer reaches abundant grace as if received from the same hands of Redeemer's Mother.

Furthermore, there is a song[28] entitled "I will open this Rosaro" (this word means Rosary in English, but it can't be translated because it's a regionalism term) which is used more commonly and brings up another symbology presented by the Rosary of Our Lady:

I will open this Rosaro	Eu vô abri este Rosaro
I will open this Rosaro	Eu vô abri este Rosaro
With God and Our Lady	Com Deus e Nossa Senhora
I will open this Rosaro	Eu vô abri este Rosaro
[...]	[...]

It appears that the word *Rosaro* is well evidenced in the chant, and it should be, perhaps, because of the existence of a plant called "tears-of-our-lady", also known as biurá. They say that Mary dealing with slavery, ached so much that she cried, and from her tears the plant was born to be made into rosaries. In Minas Gerais, Conglese and Mozambican people continue proclaiming their devotion.

The countries Congo and Mozambique were the regions of Africa from where the first African slave groups were brought to Brazil. The Arturos, traditional group from Minas Gerais, ensured that it was the lament of Mozambique which turned Mary on "Holy Mother of colored people" (Augras, 2005, p. 45):

Mozambique called me, ow, ow	Moçambique me chamô, ai, ai
In Rosaro and here I go, ow, ow	No Rosaro e eu já lá vô, ai, ai
In my mother's Rosaro, oh, guys!	No Rosaro de minha mãe, oh, gente!
Our Lady took it, ah! [29]	Nossa Senhora levô, ah!

29

---

28   *Song Eu vô abri este Rosaro* (I willl open this Rosary)
29   Ibid.

The researcher Augras (2005) adds that "The African people arrived in Brazil brought by the slave ships, but the Virgin Mary, also Queen of the sea, crossed the ocean to rescue their children." (P.45)

The numerous brotherhoods of the Rosary, whether in its strictly religious component or through the amusements that helped it to perpetuate, started to have the dual function at the same time ensuring the triumph of Catholicism and the control of slaves.

What was said above is part of one of several stories related to the existence of Our Lady of Rosary and her relationship with some people and cultures of African origin. However, there is evidently a particular fondness for the allocation of the Virgin Mary by African people. From North to South of Brazil, there are legends whose the topic is: a statue of Our Lady of the Rosary appeared on the seaside, the caboclos (In Brazil, caboclo is person of mixed Indigenous Brazilian and European ancestry) who are the first owners of the land by indigenous descent, sang and prayed, leading the statue to a chapel, but the next day, it had returned to the place where it was found. So did the sailors, representing the white Portuguese people and She either attended them. But when colored people praised, She went with them to where they wanted.

Thus, it can also be seen in the excerpts that follow, for the opening song «Virgin of the Rosary» elements linked to the Mary›s life, which refer mainly to the dogmas annunciation, the conception and the stages of Jesus› life on Earth.

Mary conceives	Maria concebe
The Verb incarnate	O verbo incarnado
Who came into the world	Que veio ao mundo
Redeem the sin.	Remir do peccado.
Feeling burned	Sentindo-se arder
All for charity	Toda em caridade
Visit Isabel	Visita Isabel
Full of humility.	Cheia de humildade.
[...]	[...]

Mary, as shown in the Gospels, inhabited by the Holy Spirit and carrying in her womb the Son of God, went to visit Elizabeth, her cousin. Before she heard the salutation of Mary, she felt her shudder child within. Full of divine love, she exclaimed aloud: "Blessed are you among women and blessed is the fruit of your womb." (Luke, 1:42). Through this greeting, it was discovered that the truth was in Mary, the incarnate Son, "the incarnate verb", who was sent into the world to free people from sin:

In the pure horizon	No puro horizonte
The sun already rising,	Já o sol nascendo,
The annunciation peace	A paz annuncião
The Angels down	Os anjos descendo
In the temple features	No templo apresenta
The boy Jesus;	A Jesus menino;
In the arms of dawn,	Nos braços da aurora,
Comes the divine sun.	Vem o Sol divino.
The child who seeks,	O filho que busca,
Full of agony,	Cheia de agonia,
In the temple finds	No templo descobre
With utmost joy.	Com summa alegria.

In the sad retreat	No triste retiro
See the child praying,	Vê o filho orando,
Of blood sweat	De suor de sangue
The land bathing.	A terra banhando.
In the strong column	Na forte columna
Already see him laced,	Já o vê atado,
An open wound	Uma chaga viva
His sacred body.	Seu corpo sagrado.
For hard thorns	Por duros espinhos
Also pierced,	Também transpassada,
The sacred Head	A sacra Cabeça
All bloody.	Toda ensangüentada.
[...]	[...]

The author shows a real intention to clarify, through the chants, the moments leading up to Jesus' death. It is true that Mary, his mother, accompanied all the events and sufferings of the Nazarene son:

The cross already being taken	A cruz já levando
In the injured shoulder,	No hombro ferido,
See falling the ground	Vê cahir por terra
The beloved son,	O filho querido,
[...]	[...]

They forced him to carry his own cross to a place called Golgotha[30]. When they saw him losing the forces, they ordered a man by the name of Simon of Cyrene, to take the cross and carry some part of the way:

He is crucified	É crucificado
Between two thieves,	Entre dous ladrões,
Die the glory King	Morre o Rei da Gloria
Full of afflictions.	Cheio de Afflicções.
[...]	[...]

---

30   This refers to the calvary.

The Son of Mary was taken outside the city and nailed to the cross by the Roman soldiers. John says that Pilate wrote on the cross, the Latin phrase, *"Iesus Nazarenus Rex Iudaeorum"*[31] The cross of Jesus was placed between two thieves. Before his death, Jesus cried out *"Eli, Eli, lama sabachthani,"* the translation means "My God, my God, why have You forsaken me?" (Matthew, 27:46):

What is the spring,	Qual a primavera,
Laughing season,	Risonha estação,
Shines the Virgin	Resplandece a Virgem
In the resurrection	Na ressurreição
[...]	[...]

After three hours nailed to the cross, Jesus died. Joseph of Arimathea and Nicodemus deposed his body in a tomb newly opened and closed with a large stone. The guards watched over the place throughout the night:

Nostalgic and joyful,	Saudosa e alegre,
Look up ascending to heaven	Vê subir ao céo
Jesus triumphant,	Jesus triumphante,
Sweet is his charm	Doce encanto seu.
The right hand of the Father	Da dextra do Padre
Your son sends	O teu filho envia
The divine Spirit	O divino Espirito
That burns to Mary.	Que abrasa a Maria.
Already leaving the land	Já deixando a terra
Mary exalted,	Maria exaltada,
To the heaven soar	Aos céos se eleva
Surrounded by angels,	Dos anjos cergada,

---

31   Jesus of Nazareth, King of the Jews (John, 19:19).

On the right of her Son	A'dextra do Filho
In throne of Glory,	Em throno de Gloria,
Crowned of light,	De luz coroada,
Already claim victory	Já canta victoria.

Do, sweet Mom,	Fazei, doce Mãi,
That in heaven too,	Que no céo tambem,
To the Jesus we pray	A Jesus louvemos
Forever. Amen.	Para sempre. Amen..

According to the Gospels, on Sunday morning, Mary Magdalene came early to the tomb of Jesus, Son of Mary, and found the stone out of place and the tomb empty. After that, the Nazarene appeared to her and to Simon Peter. Eleven faithful apostles met him, first in Jerusalem and then in Galilee where He was seen by a few hundred people. However, it is the Matthew's account that offers more details about the events surrounding the time of the resurrection. According to Matthew, Jesus' resurrection would have been preceded by a major earthquake due to the removal of the stone that was in the tomb's entrance.[32]

Even though the detailed passages of life and death of Jesus in the Bible, you can understand them through the chant very easily, causing people who use the songs as a form of worship, can approach and meet even more historical and biblical facts surrounding the life of Mary and her Son, the Nazarene.

THE SORROWFUL VIRGIN MARY

It is viewed in this epithet "The Sorrowful Virgin Mary", an allegory to Mary of Nazareth suffering with the beloved Son, Jesus Christ. The author of the hymn, unidentified, unlike the composer of the song quoted above unfolded a lot the question of the act of suffering of Mary, urging all the words when referring to the pain, distress:

---

32   HOLY BIBLE, passim.

Sorrowful Virgin,	Virgem dolorosa,
that afflicted weep,	que aflita chorais,
full of anguish,	repleta de angústias,
ye blessed!	bendita sejais!
[...]	[...]

The truths of the facts are reflected in the poetic language of the author, leading the reader to imagine the pain suffered by Holy of Nazareth through persuasive arguments, presenting Christ as a model of first cause of Mary's martyrdom .

It demonstrates, however, the anguish of the woman («Lady of Sorrows»), before the son who seeks to imitate the perfection of the Father. The composer used in the rhetoric arguments to mimic such pain by often inserting words that suggest suffering, bitterness:

Blessed ye	Bendita sejais
Lady of sorrows	Senhora das dores
Hear our woes	ouvi nossos ais
mother of sinners.	mãe dos pecadores.
[...]	[...]

The "Lady of Sorrows" is the Mary who went through the agonies of suffering and death of her son Jesus Christ. So it was her the chosen to hear the cries of Christians who, for various reasons, feel pain and cry for help.

From Simeon the voices,	De Simeão as vozes,
in the temple you should flee,	no templo fujais,
cruel prophecies,	cruéis profecias,
ye blessed!	bendita sejais!
[...]	[...]

The sentence summary about Simeon, "Now there was a man in Jerusalem whose name was Simeon, and this man was righteous and devout, waiting for the consolation of Israel, and the Holy Spirit was upon him" (Luke, 2:25), indicates that he had a path that resembled the same of Joseph in Egypt, about whom his contemporaries noted full of certainty, although they do not believe in the God of Joseph, "Pharaoh said to his servants, "Can we find anyone like this man, in whom is the Spirit of God?" (Genesis, 41:38).

As the whole ancient Israel, Simeon waited for the consolation of his people. He awaited the coming of the Messiah who would restore power to his people, that was massacred by different empires few centuries ago. The long wait has caused many to give up or to depart from the biblical vision of the Messiah.

After it has recognized in Jesus "a light for revelation to the Gentiles, and the glory of Your people Israel" (Luke, 2:32), Simeon announces to Mary the great trial to which the Messiah is called and reveals her participation in that sorrowful destiny.

This reference to the sacrifice of the Redeemer, absent at the Annunciation, made to be seen in the oracle of Simeon almost a "second notice"[33] which led the Virgin to a deeper understanding of her Son`s mystery.

The old man who, until that moment had addressed all those present, blessing Joseph and Mary in particular, now predicts only to the Virgin the ones who will participate in the fate of the Son. Then Simeon blessed them and said to Mary His mother, "Listen, this Child is destined to cause the fall and rising of many in Israel and to be a sign which will be spoken against, so that the thoughts of many hearts may be revealed. And a sword will pierce through your own soul also" (Luke 2: 34-35).

Like Mary, Simeon was patient and waited for the coming of the Messiah; the voice of this man could be heard around the temple, repelling the prophecies that were conducive to the coming of the Savior.

However, in the stretch below, there is the announcement of the passage in which it was asked to send an angel from heaven to advise the Nazarene to flee the sovereign, unjust and cruel men:

---

33   *Redemptoris Mater.*

[...]	[...]
Send an angel from heaven,	Manda do céu um anjo,
say that you should flee,	dizer que fujais,
from the tyrant servant,	do servo tirano,
ye blessed!	bendita sejais!
[...]	[...]

Mary was looking for the Nazarene in the temple, place where He used to visit to inquire and talk to men of Law; finding none, the woman of Nazareth suffered a great fright, fearing for Child Protection.

So, it is found in the stretches of the hymn at issue, dedicated to the Nazarene, an indication of the seven sorrows suffered by the Virgin: the prophecy of Simeon, the flight into Egypt, the loss of the Child Jesus in the Temple, the meeting of Jesus and Mary on the way of the Cross, the Crucifixion, Jesus is taken down from the Cross and given to his Mother, and the body of Jesus is buried:

Returning from the temple,	Voltando do templo,
You didn't find Jesus	Jesus não achais;
what a fright you suffered!	que susto sofrestes!
Blessed ye!	Bendita sejais!
A hard sword	Uma dura espada
of mortal pain,	de dores mortais,
that passes your chest,	o peito vos passa,
Blessed ye!	bendita sejais!
That unexplained pain,	Que dor inexplicável,
when you meet him,	quando o encontrais,
with the Cross on his back!	com a Cruz às costas!
Blessed ye!	Bendita sejais!

The pain is still growing,	A dor ainda cresce,
when you contemplate,	quando contemplais,
Jesus expiring!	Jesus expirando!
Blessed ye!	Bendita sejais!
In your arms,	Nos vossos braços,
His body you hold,	seu corpo abrigais,
embraced him!	com ele abraçada!
Blessed ye!	Bendita Sejais!
Without son and such Son!	Sem filho e tal Filho!
Then you endure	Então suportais
Cruel loneliness,	Cruel solidão,
Blessed ye!	bendita sejais!

This chant denotes a rich history that distributed in the verses, tries to approximate the devotee of Mary, as well as the certain existence of That One who made her "blessed." The aspirations have a key role in keeping the values that the song conveys.

MARY, MOTHER OF US ALL

Mary, mother of Jesus	Maria, mãe de Jesus
Guiding star in the sky	No céu uma estrela guia
Announced a new day	Anunciou um novo dia
And then a light shone	E uma luz então brilhou
[...]	[...]

Mary is here called the "Mother of Jesus" for having generated the only begotten son of God, foretelling thus a new day, new time signal to the people.

An angel announced	Que um anjo anunciou
That would be born	Que nasceria
The holy womb of Mary	O santo ventre de Maria
That one who would be the true love	Aquele que seria o verdadeiro amor
So much light became truth, purity	Tanta luz se fez verdade, pureza e
and goodness of the most beautiful	bondade da mais linda flor.
flower.	[...]
[...]	

The birth of the Nazarene was announced by the angel Gabriel. The womb of Mary, considered pure, would give life to that one who would be the symbol of love and Earth salvation, who would come to take away all the sin of the world.

Holy Mother of Hope of Angel child	Santa mãe da esperança do anjo
our savior	criança nosso salvador
Mary of the desperate, of the unjust,	Maria do desesperado, dos
of the suffering ones.	injustiçados, dos sofredores.
Mary of all tears, of dreams, of	Maria de todos os prantos, sonhos,
disappointments of so many pains.	desencantos de tantas dores.
Mary of John and Joseph, Queen of	Maria de João e José, rainha da fé,
faith, queen of light.	rainha de luz.
Mary, mother of us all.	Maria, mãe de todos nós.
[...]	[...]

This single passage can give us various descriptive forms for the Holy, which denotes Her presence in the social environment, lacking in justice: "Holy Mother of Hope, of Angel, of the children, our savior," "Mary of the desperate , of the unjust, of the suffering ones" "Mary of all tears, of dreams, of the disappointments, of so many sorrows "; "Mary of John and Joseph", "Queen of Faith," "Queen of Light" and "Mother of us all."

Here, it can be seen how the Mother of God is considered the liberator of the people, the one who takes care of the desperate, unjust and suffering ones in general. The Holy who looks for those who mourn, who hope and who have physical and moral sufferings. She is the blessed mother:

[...]	[...]
Blessed art thou, Jesus' mother.	Benditas sós vós, mãe de Jesus.
Blessed art thou, Jesus' mother.	Benditas sós vós, mãe de Jesus.
Blessed art thou, Jesus' mother.	Benditas sós vós, mãe de Jesus.
Guiding star in the sky	No céu uma estrela guia
Announced a new day	Anunciou um novo dia
[...]	[...]

It is possible to check on the verse above, the repetition of the word blessed, which reinforces the special status of Mary in the Christian community. She is the blessed woman, the mother of Jesus and also considered our guiding star.

In the same verse, on the use of words "art thou"[34], it appears that *art* is referring to *are*[35]. Continuing to emphasize the birth of God, of the pure heart of the Holy, the poem takes up the annunciation of the coming of Jesus through Mary:

And then a light shone	E uma luz então brilhou
And an angel announced	Que um anjo anunciou
That would be born	Que nasceria
The holy womb of Mary	O santo ventre de Maria
That one who would be the true love	Aquele que seria o verdadeiro amor
[...]	[...]

Below, the qualities of the kind and merciful Virgin are once again reminded: "Holy Mother of hope of the Angel child our savior," "Mary of the desperate ones" " of the unjust ones" "of the suffering ones" "Mary of all tears, dreams, disappointments of so many pains "and" Mary of John and Joseph ".

---

34   It is an attempt of assimilation. A contamination by assimilation makes the text becomes more poetic.

35   In portuguese the phrase "Blessed art thou, Jesus' mother." is "Benditas sós vós, mãe de Jesus" where it appears that "sós" which is referring to "sois" that in english is equivalent to "are"; in portuguese, the translation of this verb is more used in the second person plural. As the verb "sós" is close to the second person plural personal pronoun "you", this contaminates the "sois".

60

So much light became truth, purity
and goodness of the most beautiful
flower.
Holy Mother of hope of the angel
child our savior.
Mary of the desperate, of the unjust,
of the suffering ones.
Mary of all tears, dreams,
disappointments of so many pains.
Mary of John and Joseph, Queen of
faith, Queen of light.
[...]

Tanta luz se fez verdade, pureza e
bondade da mais linda flor.
Santa mãe da esperança do anjo
criança nosso salvador.
Maria do desesperado, dos
injustiçados dos sofredores.
Maria de todos os prantos, sonhos,
desencantos de tantas dores.
Maria de João e José, rainha da fé,
rainha de luz.
[...]

The exposed Virgin is the source "of purity and goodness"; there is a combination of several epithets that idealize the Holy, showing the worshiper how she, the Virgin, is close to him and reconciles skills to help him in any situation.

Mary, the mother of us all.
Blessed art thou, Jesus' mother.
Mary of the desperate, the unjust, the
suffering ones.
Mary of all tears, dreams,
disappointments of so many pains.
Mary of John and Joseph, Queen of
faith, queen of light.

Maria, mãe de todos nós.
Benditas sós vós, mãe de Jesus.
Maria do desesperado, dos
injustiçados dos sofredores.
Maria de todos os prantos, sonhos,
desencantos de tantas dores.
Maria de João e José, rainha da fé,
rainha de luz.

Mary, the mother of us all.
Blessed art thou, Jesus' mother.
Blessed art thou, Jesus' mother.
Blessed art thou, Jesus' mother.
Mother of Jesus.

Maria, mãe de todos nós.
Benditas sós vós, mãe de Jesus.
Benditas sós vós, mãe de Jesus.
Benditas sós vós, mãe de Jesus.
Mãe de Jesus.

In this sense, a Greek text was found in a papyrus that seems to belong to the Third Century, in which there is an old invocation of the Virgin, "*Sub tuum praesidium*", which may explain the "Blessed art thou" phrase dedicated to the Virgin: "Under the protection of your mercy we take refuge Oh Mother of God; do not despise our prayers in our difficulties; but deliver us from danger, only you pure (or venerated) blessed art thou [sic] "(MIEGGE, 1962, p. 141-142).

In another chant[36], "Virgin Mother, Heart of Mary," the author also draws on Mary "Blessed of the Lord", who accepted wholeheartedly the God who was generated in her womb. Welcomed in silence the message sent by the angel Gabriel, giving life to what was at first only word:

Virgin Mother, Heart of Mary, that to the Lord was entire membership, The one Blessed of the Lord, silence that hosted, the Word of the Father, the voice. [...]	Virgem Mãe, Coração de Maria, que ao Senhor foste inteira adesão, a Bendita do Senhor, silêncio que acolheu, do Pai o Verbo, a voz. [...]

According to the Gospel of Luke (1: 26-38), the angel Gabriel was sent from God unto a city of Galilee, called Nazareth, the target was to convey the message of God to a virgin who was engaged to a man whose name was Joseph, of the house of David; and the virgin's name was Mary. The angel, entering where she was, said "Hail, favored one! the Lord is with thee; blessed art thou among women." The woman was still not understanding and suffered disruptions because she did not understand what those words were. The Virgin of Nazareth said to the angel, "How can this be, see I am a virgin?" The angel answered her, "The Holy Spirit will come on you, and the

power of the Most High will overshadow you. Therefore, also the Holy One who is born from you will be called the Son of God." These passages found in the scriptures are the evidence of the time of announcing the arrival of the Son of God through Mary.

Thus, continuing, the author of the song does not end the sacrum plot; it delivers the story of the Annunciation through the hymns to the devotee:

---

36   Song Virgem Mãe, Coração de Maria (Virgin Mother, Heart of Mary)

62

That your "Just do it", embodying the impossible, open us to love, and to the earth bring the heaven: Mary, pray to God for us! [...]	Que o teu "Assim se faça", encarnando o impossível, nos abra ao amor, e a terra traga o céu: Maria, roga a Deus por nós! [...]

And Elizabeth, her cousin, conceived a son in her old age, and this is the sixth month for her who was called barren, because for God nothing is impossible. Mary said, "Behold, the servant of the Lord; let it be done to me according to your word." The angel departed from her " (Luke, 1:38).

Embracing the Father's will, you stayed closer to the brother. Give us life in complete harmony with your maternal heart. [...]	Abraçando do Pai a vontade, bem mais perto ficaste do irmão. Dá-nos viver em total sintonia com teu materno Coração. [...]

The angel said to her:

Don't be afraid, Mary, for you have found favor with God. Behold, you will conceive in your womb, and give birth to a son, and will call his name 'Jesus.' He will be great, and will be called the Son of the Most High. The Lord God will give him the throne of his father, David, and he will reign over the house of Jacob forever. There will be no end to his Kingdom. (Luke 1: 30-33).

The Holy accepted the will of God, getting closer to the brother and to the society. Mary's consent was the milestone for the harmony between God and man. The maternal heart of the Holy enabled an eternal divine bond.

MOTHER

The composer «To comfort Mary,» mentions as it was stated in other previous excerpts, the episode of the crucifixion and death of Jesus. Mary his mother, according to the Scriptures, accompanied all the way done by the Son, until he was killed on the cross:

It was a long day in Jerusalem along the cross, Mary: so sad, I did not see anyone else. [...]	Ia longe o dia em Jerusalém, junto a cruz, Maria: tão triste, não vi mais ninguém. [...]
I want, Maria, to be your Jesus[37], even if one day I could die on the cross. [...]	Quero, Maria, ser teu Jesus, mesmo que um dia morra na cruz. [...]

The suffering of Mary to see the Son, considered by many Christians as the savior of the world, dying to death was immense, only a mother with much love and comforted by the Spirit of God could stand to suffer as she suffered. The author of the poem sees himself as the son of the Saint, even if he died crucified like Jesus. The composer shows himself disposed to suffer as Jesus suffered. Is the author's intention to put himself in Jesus's life? He could tell similar:

How much pain you felt, Mother, while contemplated thy dear Jesus, on the cross to pay my sin. [...]	Quanta dor sentias, Mãe, ao contemplar teu Jesus querido, na cruz meus pecados pagar. [...]

The Virgin, suffering and crying, saw her Son, Jesus, left the earthly world to "save the sins of the world." She was strong enough to resist the insults and cruel punishments that the Son has received on the cross, as the evangelists say.

The wonder here is for the courage and moral resistance that Mary had in face of the situation in which she was submitted. She is the symbol of woman honored and chosen by God, the one who did not let it falter in the most tolerable moments:

---

37   Being your Jesus is a metaphor. Similar to the Mater Dolorosa is a declaration of surrender that is unorthodox, it is a mere poetic expression. He changed the general (son) by the particular (Jesus).

Since that day I have never met, someone like Mary, so sad, I didn't even seen anyone else.	Desde aquele dia jamais encontrei, ser igual Maria, tão triste, nem vi mais ninguém.

According to Miegge (1962, p. 179), the presence and the pain of Mary give to the passion of Christ a great intensity and, above all, a human quality which would miss her deeply. The sufferings of Mary would be missed in a redemption that wants to be the offering to God of all human pain. Jesus could suffer anything but compassion for their own suffering.

GRACED MOTHER

If one day an angel said, that you were full of God; Now I think: who am I, to not tell you also, full of grace, oh Graced Mother [...]	Se um dia um anjo declarou, que tu eras cheia de Deus; agora penso: quem sou eu, para não te dizer também, cheia de graça, ó Mãe Agraciada [...]

In this chant it can be seen that the Holy is recalled, worshiped as usual. The author puts himself on the poem, obviously with the intention of representing the devotees of the Saint, as the Marian pity is one of the most impressive aspects of the contemporary Catholic devotion. The epithets "full of grace" and "Graced Mother" are very well placed in the chant, because they denote the true gift of the Holy.

The "woman clothed with the sun", indicated in the following passage refers to the Immaculate, which appears as a tender woman and at the same time warrior that crushing the serpent's head; the image combines features of the woman clothed with the sun (Revelation 12: 1-2) and traces of proto-evangelium woman (Genesis 1:15):

It appeared a great sign from heaven: A woman clothed with the sun, the moon under her feet, and on her head a crown There's nothing to compare with, perfect is the one who created you, if the Creator crowned you. [...]	Surgiu um grande sinal do céu: uma mulher revestida de sol, a lua debaixo de seus pés, e na cabeça uma coroa Não há com que se comparar, perfeito é quem te criou, se o Criador te coroou. [...]

The Holy is worthy of being crowned, she is the mother of the creator, the queen of all peoples. To receive the crown is necessary to be worthy of the people's worship, Mary had these qualities, and therefore that one who's worthy of devotions:

We crowned you, oh Mother, We crowned you, oh Mother, Our queen.	Te coroamos, ó Mãe, te coroamos, ó Mãe, Nossa Rainha

GLORIOUS LADY

Glorious Lady, you shine brighter more than sun. The God who created you to the breast you nurse [...]	Senhora gloriosa, bem mais que o sol brilhais. O Deus que vos criou ao seio amamentais. [...]

The glorious lady who shines brighter than the sun, is the Virgin who is bright and at all times is graced. The same God who created the Holy is the one who gave her the honor of being the mother of Jesus, the one who came, according to the scriptures, to take away the sins of the world.

[...] What Eve destroyed, in the son you recreate; Of the heaven you open the door and the sad ones you hold. [...]	[...] O que Eva destruiu, no filho recriais; do céu abris a porta e os tristes abrigais. [...]

It is noticed in this stretch that there is an antithesis which establishes the relationship of the figure of Mary and Eve, this was the image of the sinful and disobedient woman and, therefore ordered to "suffer the pains of childbirth". It can be found at the figure of Mary the Saint model who allowed the graces came by God, being given the task of becoming the Mother of Jesus Christ (Pagels, 1992).

What Eve, the first woman created by God from Adam›s rib, destroyed, by disobedience, the Virgin Mary recreated, opening the gates of heaven to house those who are devoid of joy.

[...]	[...]
From the bright door light,	Da luz brilhante porta,
ye porch of the King.	sois pórtico do Rei.
From the Virgin came the life.	Da virgem veio a vida.
Redeemed, bless!	Remidos, bendizei!
[...]	[...]

Here there is another mention of the main door of heaven. For the author of the poem, there is a guardian that controls the entrance, who releases the passage of those who will be received by King, this protector is the Mother of God, the lady who gave life to Jesus of Nazareth.

In this sense, it's also possible locate in one of the poems of the medieval poet Gonzalo de Berceo (1964) an analogy to the ideas of the chant above. The text of the poet also refers to the Virgin as the guardian, that one who takes care of the entrance and exit, the one who "everyone" must consult, or rather she is a guard that protects the front door. In his words: "[...] Ella es dicha puerto a qui todos corremos, / E puerta por la qual entrada atendemos. / Ella es dicha puerta, em si bien encerrada, / Pora nos es abierta, pora darnos la entrada."[38]

---

38   She is the happiness of the port to which we all run; She is the door through which we entered; She is the gate, which is firmly closed; To us is open, so we can get in. "(Our translation).

Considering the poem of Berceo, written in medieval times, and other sacred compositions that can be seen throughout this research, it is possible to admit that many songs used in today's Catholic churches have many similarities to the chants produced with ideas from previous centuries.

HAIL OF SEA STAR

In this chant[39], in which the author calls the Virgin "Hail of Sea Star", It can infer that the title is related to "Our Lady of Navigators". She is compared to the "Star of the Sea", the one who protects the navigators, showing them the best shelter and the port of salvation.

It is also important to remember that at the beginning of the century the ships were guided following the position of the stars, being these the essential elements to guide navigation on the high seas (POLÓNIA, 2003). So Mary is compared to the principal "Star" that guides mariners in every way:

Hail of Sea Star	Ave do mar Estrela,
Blessed Mother of God,	bendita Mãe de Deus,
fruitful and ever Virgin,	fecunda e sempre Virgem,
happy portal of heaven.	portal feliz dos céus.
[...][40]	[...]

To Megale (2001) this comparison started during the Middle Ages (crusades), when Christians crossed the Mediterranean in the Palestinian demands to defend the holy places of the desecration of the infidels. Mariners had in memory the reminder of the terrible sea crossings to the fragile vessels of the time faced. Therefore they resorted to Mary's care.

Even as the words of Nilza Megale (2001), in the time of sailing, this devotion has developed greatly between the Portuguese and Spanish navigators, who ventured into the unknown ocean. Before the departure of vessels, travelers attended mass and implored the protection of the Mother of navigators on

---

39   Song Ave do mar Estrela (Hail of Sea Star)
40   Ibid.

journeys overseas. It is known that Christopher Columbus called "Santa Maria" one of his caravels and Pedro Alvares Cabral, during the voyage of discovery, brought (in the ship) an image of Our Lady of Hope.

> [...] As natural, soon arrived in Brazil the devotion of the seamen under the various titles given to the Heavenly Patroness: Lady of the Seas, of the Good Voyage, of the Navigators, etc. This last invocation was most used by fishermen, modest men who daily faced the fury of the waves in search of support themselves and their families; proof of this is that the most famous shrines of Our Lady of the Navigators in our country are situated in fisheries areas, as in Mucuripe Beach in Fortaleza (Ceará); in Penedo (Alagoas) at the mouth of the River; in Porto Alegre in Rio Grande do Sul; in addition to Santos and Cananéia, on the coast of São Paulo region. (Megale, 2001).

It's possible to observe that the Holy in a single stretch of the chant indicated earlier in this analysis is called "Hail of Sea Star", "blessed mother of God," "fruitful and ever Virgin" and "happy portal of heaven." These are four types of descriptions that emphasize the greatness of the Mother of God.

The nouns *sea* and *star*, found in the chant "Hail Sea Star" have a drive relationship with one of the poems of the medieval poet Gonçalo de Berceo, who belonged to another time and culture. However, it is possible to find in some troubadour poems in question, a reference to foreigners who sailed in search of new land. The protection that they chose to have success in the navigations was almost often the protection of Mary, as can be seen in the excerpt:

> *La bendicta Virgen es* estrella *clamada,* /Estrella de los mares, *guïona deseada,* / *Es de los marineros en las cuitas guardada,* / *Ca quando essa veden, es la nave guiada.*/ *Es clamada e eslo de los cielos, reyna,* / *Tiemplo de Jesus Cristo,* estrella matutina / *Sennora natural, pïadosa vezina,* / *De cuerpos e de almas salud e medicina.*[41] (BERCEO 1964, p. 9, emphasis added).

---

41   "The Blessed Virgin is requested star; starfish, of the sea, desired guide; she is the protector of sailors at work; here when she comes, she guides the ship; She is acclaimed, and she reigns the heaven of heavens, the queen; Temple of Jesus Christ, the morning star; Lady of nation, pious neighbor; body and soul is health and medicine. "(our translation).

In this poem of Berceo, as well as other poems sung in some Catholic churches in Brazil, there are some pieces of evidence found in the "protector saint of navigators", "star of the sea", the "Our Lady of the navigators".

Berceo says that "Blessed Virgin" is the claimed star, so "star of the sea", the "desired guide for all", being her the "eagerness saved of sailors" because she is the one who guides the ship, she is also called the "Queen of Heaven,"

"Temple of Jesus Christ" and "Morning Star". In this poem, the Virgin is also considered "Lady of all nation" and "pitying neighbor." In conclusion, the Holy is for the author, synonymous of health and medicine for the body and soul.

These descriptions of treatment found in the poem in question are very close to the epithets found in the Marian texts today. Some sacred contemporary authors allude to the Virgin "Star" and "guide seas", perhaps because they are familiar with the poems and songs brought to Brazil at the beginning of colonization.

Another example of the Holy "guide of the Seas" in the song number 20 can be inserted, "A thousand times admirable Mary," in which the epithet "Star of the Sea" appears showing a Mary endowed with grace and extending hands to guide the devotees. The feminine noun Mary appears written all in capital letters, reinforcing the admiration given to the Saint:

A thousand times admirable MARY,	Mil vezes admirável MARIA,
beautiful mother, holy mother.	mãe bela, mãe santa.
You are the Sea Star that guides us!	Tu és a Estrela do Mar que nos guia!
What a source of grace, extend your hand,	Qual fonte de graças, estende tuas mãos,
pour yourself out into blessings on our floor.	derrama-te em bençãos sobre nosso chão.
A thousand times because of joy,	Mil vezes causa de alegria,
of those who entrust to your heart	de quem se confia ao teu Coração,
Mary, Mary	Maria, Maria
[...]	[...]

This Holy "Star of the Sea" is also related to the first woman, Eve, in the moment when a message was left by the Angel Gabriel, which can be viewed in the chant below:

Hearing that Hail	Ouvindo aquele Ave
said by the Angel Gabriel,	do anjo Gabriel,
changing the name of Eve,	mudando de Eva o nome,
bring us peace of heaven.	trazei-nos paz do céu.
[...]	[...]

The historic pair Eve and Mary is for now remembered in songs and prayers intended for the Virgin of Nazareth. The memory of the first woman created by God, through Adam›s rib, presents a considered visibility when it comes to fall and redemption, and that word meant to Eve and this refers to Mary.

The researcher Mieggue (1962) says, following the thought of St. Irenaeus, that Mary rehabilitates Eve or defends her cause, or even console her. It is observed in an apocryphal Gospel that Eve goes to the cave of Bethlehem to attend her redemptive. There is no indication that St. Irenaeus later allegorize parallelly and have a look at Eve as a symbol of natural humanity, and Mary as the universal mother of sinners, or the Church's image. This famous parallel gives the impression of an ingenious literary construction, more than an intentional theological doctrine.

Also according to Mieggue:

> [...] The parallel of Eve and Mary in St. Bernard receives a broad and lyrical modulation: "A man and a woman made us a great evil, he exclaims in a sermon on Sunday that follows the feast of the Assumption of Mary; but, thank God, by means of a man and a woman, everything was remedied ... The prudent and merciful craftsman did not destroy what was damaged, but remade it throughout in the most useful way: the old Adam formed the new and transformed Eve in Mary [...] (1962, p. (142)

And he goes on to say that,

> [...] We need a mediator for this mediator and none will be more useful than Mary. Eve was a cruel mediator through which that old serpent infused in man a pestiferous poison; but faithful is Mary that gave men the salutary antidote. That one was for us Minister of seduction, and this one propitiation; the one who suggests the dereliction of duty and this one who introduces redemption. Why does the frail humanity fear of approaching Mary? There is nothing austere, nothing terrible; she is all smooth and she offers all milk and wool. (MIEGGUE, 1962, p. 142).

Continuing to the hymn sung by Sister Miria Kolling (2003), it's possible to see that Mary, as well as all attributive adjuncts mentioned above, has qualities that promote his holiness, enlighten the blind, free the defendants of all evil, keep people and offers all good:

To the blind enlighten,	Ao cego iluminai,
to the defendant set him free also;	ao réu livrai também;
of all evil beware us	de todo mal guardai-nos
and give us all good.	e dai-nos todo o bem.

She showed to be our Mother,	Mostrai ser nossa Mãe,
taking our voice	levando a nossa voz
to Who, born for us,	a Quem, por nós nascido,
deigned come from you.	dignou-se vir de vós.

There is an appeal to the Virgin Mary that shows she is really the chosen to be the mother of the people, " the protector". She claims and requests from the people to God, who "was born to save us", who is worthy to have come from the womb of Mary.

Softer than all,	Suave mais que todas,
Oh Virgin unique	ó Virgem sem igual
make us meek, pure,	fazei-nos mansos, puros,
guard us against evil.	guardai-nos contra o mal.

The Holy, "soft more than all", is a different virgin of other pure women, because she is the blessed mother and full of grace. In the poem, the Holy is asked to intervene in the devotee life, making him meek, pure, and keeping him from evil.

Oh! Give us pure life,	Oh! dai-nos vida pura,
guide us to the light,	guiai-nos para a luz,
and one day, at your side,	e um dia, ao vosso lado,
we can see Jesus.	possamos ver Jesus.
[...]	[...]

Thus, through these verses, there has been a fervent belief in the Holy wonders. There is a claim for pure life and follow-up to the light; the Virgin is a star that through her light, she reflects the light of Christ (MENDEZ apud AZEVEDO, 2001). She has divine powers that is able to guide people to the light.

Azevedo (2001, p. 32) points out that Mary accompanies the people in "exile" and "loneliness", in the "pain" and "death." She goes with them everywhere and gives them hope: with her "help", with her "advices", with her "consolation".

She helps and sustains, guides and rescues, gives remedy to those who are sick and breaks free, she leads to "victory" and introduces "glory". As mentioned in the opening paragraphs, it's noted that the Holy is the one who came to liberate the people from all the anxieties and persecutions; a poor woman, but aware of her importance, being this the world that the people identified themselves with and that can not be ignored.

FROM CHARITY SHINING STAR

The indicated chant, of unknown author and collected from the book "Liturgy of the Hours" [42] presents in its content a wistful prayer to the Saint from Nazareth.

Mary once again, in another chant, is described as a Star, "Shining Star", owning too bright, which is in the words of the poem, to the divine inhabitants, she is also the "hope" and "source of bubbling water. "

From Charity Shining Star
to the heavenly inhabitants,
for mortals thou art hope
the source of bubbling water.
[...]

Da caridade Estrela fúlgida
para os celestes habitantes,
para os mortais és da esperança
a fonte de águas borbulhantes.
[...]

---

42   It is the official public and communal prayer of the Catholic Church, also called the Divine Office. The word Office comes from the Latin opus meaning work. Basically consists of daily prayer in varied times of the day, through Psalms and hymns, reading scriptures and the elevation of prayers to God.

Also called the "Noble Lady", the Holy is considered powerful because she has the Son (Jesus Christ) in her heart, and thus who pray confident in her powers, can get the eternal salvation of God. The Holy is considered the intermediary between man and God:

Noble Lady, thou art powerful of the Son on the heart; for you, who prays, confident, of him achieves salvation. [...]	Nobre Senhora, és poderosa do Filho sobre o coração; por ti, quem ora, confiante, dele consegue a salvação. [...]

Boff says that usually the theology and piety have associated strongly Mary to Jesus, and discusses both are united in the same destiny and the same salvific function. There are good reasons for this, whether biblical or theological: Mary is venerated as co-redemptrix, mediatrix of all graces, Universal Queen (BOFF, L., 1990).

In the following excerpt, it is observed that the goodness of the Mother of God serves not only the voice of the supplicants, anticipating even the most uncertain desires. The words of eternal exaltation to the Holy are linked to the different values given to her and only her,

Your kindness not only meets the voice of the supplicants, but anticipates, caring, to their hesitant desires. [...]	Tua bondade não apenas atende a voz dos suplicantes, mas se antecipa, carinhosa, aos seus desejos hesitantes. [...]

The Virgin is named "Mercy" for the greatness that she reveals. The goodness of the Holy quenches people, and it is this goodness that makes devotees come ever closer to the figure of Mary of Nazareth:

Mercy is your name,	Misericórdia é o teu nome,
such greatness in you shines.	suma grandeza em ti fulgura.
With alive water of kindness,	Com água viva de bondade,
satiate every creature.	saciais toda a criatura.
[...]	[...]

Mieggue (1962) says that while the fourth century pays special attention to the virginity of Mary, from the fifth to the seventh centuries are dedicated to her divine motherhood, the time Carolingian to her assumption, the twelfth to fourteenth centuries to her Immaculate Conception and the time extending from the Council of Trent to the French Revolution, which deals especially on set, reacting against the Reformation, Jansenism and the Enlightenment, the universal mediation and merciful motherhood of Mary.

MARY, OH MOTHER FULL OF GRACE

Mary, oh mother full of grace,	Maria, ó mãe cheia de graça,
Mary protects your children,	Maria protege os filhos teus,
Mary, Mary, we want	Maria, Maria, nós queremos
Be with you in heaven.	contigo estar nos céus.
[...]	[...]

In this chant, Mary is called "mother full of grace". Mary is asked here to protect the children, and the Virgin to be present on the day the devotees are dead in heaven. There is a huge desire evidenced in most songs, that Mary is present at the time of death and after this event.

Leonardo Boff (1990) writes the following text about the Virgin endowed with grace:

> Now we empower ourselves to understand the angel's greeting to Mary: "Hail, full of grace; the Lord is with thee; blessed be thou among women" (Lk 1:28). We can notice that the angel Gabriel does not use the name Mary; he replaces the name Mary by true name she has in God's plan: that one of being the contemplated becoming the temple of the Holy Spirit. The Greek term is Kecharitomene that

translated means: the gratified, the privileged, the contemplated, that one who was made object of God's love. St. Jerome in the Vulgate translated by full of grace (gratia plena); this translation is correct, but insufficient; it misses the deeper sense of the mystery of Mary. By the expression 'full of grace' our attention is thrown on the inside and full grace of Mary; We contemplate the unprecedented fact that Mary was already inhabited by the Holy Spirit. We emphasize the effect, exalt the greatness of Mary. This view is correct; but it is not the first nor the most fundamental [...] (p. 44)

Therefore, the Virgin is considered "full of grace" and is also, according to Leonardo Boff, the contemplated for being taken as the temple of the Holy Spirit. The Holy is gratified and privileged to have been chosen by God among women and the one who shows conditions to route people, whether in life or in death.

In this sense, it is found in hymn: "With my mother I will be" such qualifications of Mary, seen as protector and carrier of souls to heaven:

In heaven, in heaven	No céu, no céu
With my mother I will be	Com minha mãe estarei.
With my mother I will be	Com minha mãe estarei
One day in the holy glory	Na santa gloria um dia
With the Virgin Mary	Juncto a Virgem Maria
In heaven I will triumph	No céo triumpharei
[...]	[...]

The whole sense of this hymn presents an approach to the reality of death. Most often it is heard such music at funerals and sacred rites, which necessarily depicts the end of life softened by the hope of protection of the Virgin Mary.

By the fragment indicated, it is apparent that the idea of forgiveness is in evidence. The sins are remembered, and even with the care of Mary, there is a desire to go through death through the Virgin and especially Jesus, "the only one" who can forgive sins:

With my mother I will be	Com minha mãe estarei
But since I have offended	Mas já que hei offendido
Your dear Jesus	Ao seu Jesus querido
I will cry because of my faults	As culpas chorarei
[...]	[...]

The author here gives the desire to be with Mary when death comes. He imagines the events in the sky, "the angels gathered me and the hymn chanting," as if the angels were waiting for him, because being a son of Mary the protection is almost certain:

With my mother I will be	Com minha mãe estarei
Good Words,	Palavras deliciosas,
That in labor-hours	Que em horas trabalhosas
Faithful I will remember	Fiel recordarei
With my mother I will be	Com minha mãe estarei
The angels gathered me	Aos anjos me ajuntando
And the hymns chanting	E hynnos entoando
I will give you praise	Louvores lhe darei
[...]	[...]

With my mother I will be	Com minha mãe estarei
While in this exile	Enquanto neste exilio
Of your godly assistance	Do seu piedoso auxilio
with faith I will prevail	com fé me valerei
With my mother I will be	Com minha mãe estarei
So worthy crown	Então corôa digna
Of your benign hand	Da sua mão benigna
Happy I will receive it	Feliz receberei

In the following fragment, the author of the hymn, diverting the attention given to Mary for her Son, "our Lord," demonstrates a desire to be in heaven, rejoicing with the Lord, knowing that the time (of death) arrives and one day the desire to get along with God will be accomplished:

Oh, I wish I could be now, partying in heaven our Lord, but I know my turn will come, and then happy I will sing your praise. [...]	Ah, quem me dera poder estar agora, festejando lá no céu nosso Senhor, mas sei que chega a minha hora, e então, feliz cantarei o seu louvor. [...]

This hymn is often sung at funerals, at the source of the body towards the place of burial.

MARY OF NAZARETH

The Holy is called "Mary of Nazareth" because the city of Nazareth, near the Mediterranean Sea of Galilee, in northern Palestine (LARRAÑAGA,1980), it is where the Virgin Mary lived and where Christ (whose birth took place in Bethlehem) was raised. The researchers Leonardo Boff and Clodovis Boff described it as:

> Mary of Nazareth, the woman of people, who watched the popular religious customs of the time ... who cared about the son ... and followed him until before the Holy Cross...Because it is so common and not because of that, Mary is all what faith proclaims that she is ... (BOFF; BOFF, 1985).

That qualifier name given to Mary is very important because it refers to the place where the Mother of Jesus lived. However It can classify it as an assignment epithet, since the term is attributed to her taking into account the region where Mary moved.

Thus, through this hymn the religious people understand, more and more, the history and life of the saint and her Son Jesus. It's a very simple hymn, but it presents a wealth of data highly appreciated by the devotees.

| Mary of Nazareth, Mary has captivated me. Made my faith stronger and as a son adopted me. Sometimes I stop and think and without realizing it when least expected I pray and my heart starts to sing to the Virgin of Nazareth. Girl who God loved and chose to be the Mother of Jesus, the Son of God. Mary that the whole people elected lady and mother of heaven. [...] | Maria de Nazaré, Maria me cativou. Fez mais forte a minha fé e por filho me adotou. Às vezes eu paro e fico a pensar e sem perceber me vejo a rezar e meu coração se põe a cantar pra Virgem de Nazaré. Menina que Deus amou e escolheu pra Mãe de Jesus, o Filho de Deus. Maria que o povo inteiro elegeu senhora e mãe do céu. [...] |

In the poem, it is clear that the "Mary of Nazareth" is that one who captivates people[43], that makes the faith become stronger and clear. The composer of the poem also considers himself as "adopted" and hosted by the Mother of God.

There is an intense praise to the Holy, the author surrenders himself to her, "Sometimes I stop and think, and without realizing it when least expected I pray, and my heart starts to sing to the Virgin of Nazareth." The moment of sacrifice seems to be only of the one who sings.

Through this chant, the author managed to make the poem circulated in various homes of "worshipers" of the Holy and God. The words are simple and easy to understand for the devotee, making them understand and get closer to the hymns more easily.

Based on the transcribed fragments, it is observed how Mary is chanted with excellence by the author of the hymn. The Holy is called "Mary of pure love", that one who is unique and "no one like you, pure mother of my Lord":

---

43   Cf. also the words of Forte (1991).

[...]	[...]
Mary that I care for,	Maria que eu quero bem,
Mary of pure love,	Maria do puro amor,
no one like you, pure mother of my Lord.	igual a você ninguém, Mãe pura do meu Senhor.
In every woman created by the earth	Em cada mulher que a terra criou
a trace of God Mary left,	um traço de Deus Maria deixou,
a mother's dream Mary planted,	um sonho de mãe Maria plantou,
to the world find peace.	pro mundo encontrar a paz.
Mary who did Christ speak,	Maria que fez o Cristo falar,
Mary who did Jesus walk,	Maria que fez Jesus caminhar,
Mary who only lived for her God,	Maria que só viveu pra seu Deus,
Mary of my people.	Maria do povo meu.

The epithets directed to Mary are estimated amounts, titles of spiritual nobility, which denote that Mary is a woman who is "above all other women," of saints and angels, being second only to God. In this sense, the researcher Giovanni Miegge (1962: 189) states that:

> [...] Mary is decorated with other titles reserved to Christ in the New Testament: she is like Christ head of our salvation, Kefalaion soterias, (George of Nicomedia, James Monaco), saving the world (Anselm, Bonaventure, Albert the Great), mercy (hilasterion) for our sins (office of Lent), liberating the death, winner of death (Gregory of Neocesarea), reconciliation of God to men (John Damaceno, Liturgy), a mediator between God and men.She has all the right to all of this because she participates with maternal and spiritual intimacy in all the works of Christ, she knows in advance the sacrifice that she will have to crown and accepts it suffering with Him spiritually at the cross [...]

OH SWEET NAME

Considering the veneration of Mary, in the previous chant, in another hymn[44] there is also a consecration of the Saint, as the author shows the skills of the Virgin of comfort and save people.

The vocative Mary, Mary! expresses how much the Holy is announced and proclaimed by the devotee, who claims to be her hope, joy; this name (Mary) will be on the lips even at death moment. Again, there is the verb die that is related to the person of Mary that is remembered in the agonizing moments of people:

Oh sweet name, Mary, Mary! Our hope, our joy! On the lips always until the death your sweet name I will bring [...]	Ó doce nome, Maria, Maria! Nossa esperança, nossa alegria! Nos lábios sempre até morrer teu doce nome hei de trazer [...]

In another section of the poem, the author calls Mary "Mother", approaching further the Saint in order to achieve greater affection to her. He asks consolation through spiritual flames received from God. And she, Mary, she is the hope, the love and the guide that leads the faithful to "the Lord"

Come Mary, oh Mother, comfort us, with your flames, come burn us. You are the hope, you are our love, You are our guide for the Lord. [...]	Vinde Maria, ó Mãe, consolar-nos, com vossas chamas, vinde abrasar- nos. Sois a esperança, sois nosso amor, sois nossa guia para o Senhor. [...]

---

44   Song Maria de Nazaré (Mary of Nazareth)

It is noticed in this other song, "To you I come to offer" the same intention to find solace and guide in the previous poem:

To you I come to offer, Lady, my love, and so I consecrate to my life to the flower. [...]	A ti venho ofertar, Senhora, o meu amor, e assim te consagrar da minha vida a flor. [...]

The love is offered to Mary; it can be seen a way of getting closer to many sentimental values. The noun *flower* also features the purity and femininity of Mary.

It should be noted here the love transferred to the Virgin Mary, the author's desire to live worshiping the Saint, and loving her, he also wants to die and rest in the mother's arms of "Mother of God", which is also called "benign":

I desire living on you, only love you, and in your mother's arms I want to die and rest.	Anseio em ti viver, a ti somente amar, e em teus braços maternos morrer e descansar.
Your Heart is Virgin, heavenly refuge. So open it, benign, to the deadly miserable.	Teu Coração é Virgem, refúgio celestial. Abri-o, pois, benigna ao mísero mortal.
You are our steps of the compass and light, the bright star that to the port leads us. [...]	Tu és dos nossos passos a bússola e a luz, a estrela fulgurante que ao porto nos conduz. [...]

Mary is therefore classified as "Lady", a woman who exercises power, domination and influence in the lives of devotees. She is considered "the steps to the compass and the light," that is, she determines the ways to make people come to the light, opening passages to bring others to God.

In this last stretch, the Virgin is placed as a real comfort, relief from the bitterness of life. The author puts himself as in the previous stanza, in the arms of the Virgin, always wanting to be with her, even after death:

Our comfort is You, pure Virgin,	Nosso conforto sois Vós, Virgem
Our relief at all bitterness.	pura,
In your life we want to be,	Nosso alívio em toda amargura.
in heaven always live with you.	Vossos na vida queremos ser,
	no céu convosco sempre viver.

Faced with these terms related to the idea that Mary accompanies people to death, and to examine the songs that address this issue, it is clear that certain coincidences are responsible for the similarity that approach them. In addition to having the same intentions, the words that suggest the idea that monitoring of Mary by the death valleys are always highlighted.

It is noted, further, that the obtained syntactic symmetry plane, since the attributes in question prior to the respective epithets. It can not lose sight of another coincidence, now on the semantic level because not only the quality but also the substances belong to the same significant fields. This phenomenon reinforces the impression just mentioned, that poetry language, among other particularities, characterized it by using binary combinations in which certain attributes attached, with variations, the same names, entailing thereby maintaining certain alliances.

Thus, taking into account the attributes for the transition to the "other life", involving the protection of Mary, Leonardo Boff (1990) presents the following argument:

> Sin accompanies us like a dark shadow, every moment, until the time of death. In this situation we need more than ever the intercession of Mary. From the glory that she accompanies maternally every child. Her kind look proves to be stronger than the dynamism of sin. That's why the pity worship her, rightly, as a co-redeemer and universal queen. Effectively there are no obstacles that stand in the way of her kind gesture; but we feel her poison distilled by every fiber of our

personal and social life. It's from it the importance through which we supplicate Mary to complete in us from generation to generation, her victory, now in every moment and especially in the supreme moment of life, the time of death. We don't need to consider death as the *terribilium terrribilissimum*, the most terrible of terrible moments; since Jesus died on the cross and rose again, since Mary participated in this human fortune and in glory was assumed into heaven, the death was dramatized and turned into the anteroom of life. However, in the death it provides a unique condition for each person: it can make your last and final synthesis of life; it can encompass everything on an act of love that gives itself the supreme mystery and set its eternal journey toward God. Right now we are alone before God, descended into our hell; we will make that decision, we will say that word that will define us forever. For this time, we pray the presence of Mary and Jesus. They will go with us, Mary as a Mother and Jesus as Brother, to the ends of our hell. So no need to fear. What we have to fear when we feel snug in mother's arms? Who feels threatened when supported by the biggest Brother? [...] (BOFF, L., 1990, p. 95-96).

It is noted here one of the reasons why several authors of Marian hymns adorn their songs with words that denote a great appreciation of the protective and welcoming being of the Virgin Mary. Through the chants, it is possible

to build on the maternal aspect that the Holy was at the cross when she accompanied her son Jesus being crucified and killed.

About the same theme, Coyle (1999) stated that in a particular scene Mary and the beloved disciple, John, are objects of the last instructions of Jesus. Both of them are witness to the meaning of Jesus' death that before his death said: "Woman, behold your son" and to the disciple whom he loved, "Behold your mother", with these two sentences that have a wide range of symbolic meaning.

The miracle at Cana[45] prepared the presentation of Mary, by the evangelist in the time of death and glorification of Jesus. The Seventh Sign[46] begins by stating that the mother of Jesus was actually standing near the cross, along with the other women (John 19:25).

Still with Coyle (1999):

> Mary was not only witness to the death of Jesus. As his mother, his death on the cross - and the pain she felt - were marked in her memory for life. When Jesus therefore had received the vinegar, He said, "It is finished." And He bowed His head and gave up the ghost (John 19:30), symbolic sentence of gift of the Spirit to his followers. She witnessed the effects of his death that brought the Spirit promised to the community, the community of the beloved disciple whose she will be mother now. As the one who remembers the death of Jesus, she will be the bearer of tradition and her presence in the community will be continuous signal of the mission and death of Jesus [...] (p. 34-35)

Therefore, it is well accepted that the authors of songs and poems in devotion to the Virgin make melodies, highlighting, in many cases, an intermediary Mary and companion at the time of death.

MY LADY

In song called "Consecration to Our Lady", quite common among Catholic because it's a high chant degree of acceptance by the devotees, an intense sense of ownership can be seen with respect to the Mother of God. The

---

45   Regarding the first miracle by Jesus, at the request of Mary. He turned water into wine for the wedding continued: "This beginning of his signs Jesus did in Cana of Galilee, and revealed his glory; and his disciples believed in him." (John 2: 1-11).

46   The seven signs are: 1) the Wedding at Cana; 2) the child's healing of a royal official; 3) healing on day feast of the Jews in Bethesda; 4) the multiplication of the breads; 5) the man's healing on the Saturday; 6) the raising of Lazarus; and 7) the great time of Jesus, his mother, the cross, the blood and water that came out on the side of Jesus (GIRARD 1980 cited GRASSI , 1988, p 73).

author makes use of several possessive pronouns to attest that the Holy is indeed his and "our" "mother". The epithets noted in the following sections are: "my Lady" and "my mother":

Oh my Lady and also my Mother, I offer myself entirely to you, And in proof of my devotion, Today I give you my heart. [...]	Ó minha Senhora e também minha Mãe, eu me ofereço inteiramente todo a Vós, E em prova da minha devoção, Eu hoje vos dou meu coração. [...]

In the following excerpt, the author devotes the eyes, the ears and the mouth to the Virgin for protection and consecration. He "surrenders" himself to the Mother of God in order to get a shelter, "guard me," "defend me," and as something "of your property," the author is entirely under the care of Mary.

I consecrate to you my eyes, my ears, my mouth, All I am I wish to You belongs Incomparable Mother, guard me, defend me As something of your property, Amen As something of your property, Amen. [...]	Consagro a vós meus olhos, meus ouvidos, minha boca, Tudo o que sou desejo que à Vós pertença Incomparável Mãe, guardai-me, defendei-me Como coisa e propriedade vossa, Amém Como coisa e propriedade vossa, Amém. [...]

Intentions similar to instances of that fragment can be seen also in chant 18, "To you Mary I consecrate myself":

Guide my life, my smile and my look! What I can and what I am all I want to consecrate! [...]	Orienta a minha vida, meu sorriso e meu olhar! O que posso e o que sou tudo quero consagrar! [...]

The author seeks a way to be closer to Mary; asks her life orientation, smile and look. The author and his ability to achieve something is also devoted to the Holy:

What I have and what I give,	O que tenho e o que dou,
my path and my walk.	meu caminho e meu andar.
What I can and what I am	O que posso e o que sou
all I want to consecrate!	tudo quero consagrar!
[...]	[...]

It is noticed that there is a surrender by the devotee of what he has, what he gives, the paths taken, the walk. Mary has, according to some authors of songs, all predicates to carry out orders that are highlighted here:

My mouth and heart,	Minha boca e coração,
hands that want to share.	mãos que querem partilhar.
What I can and what I am	O que posso e o que sou
all I want to consecrate!	tudo quero consagrar!

It is consecrated the mouth of the devotee, the heart and the "hands that want to share. "The Virgin, in the Christian tradition, presents unimaginable values that make the religious come closer to her in the search for various types of aid or spiritual healing related to body and health.

It can be seen in this another hymn[47] Mary being described as a "dear Mother" and an equal dedication of love:

Here we have seen, dear Mother,	Aqui vimos, Mãe querida,
Consecrate to you our love.	Consagrar-te o nosso amor.
[...]	[...]

There is also a demonstration of a mother, which was once loving and then presents the Holy with warrior qualities, all «beautiful and immaculate» that crushing poisoned head of the dragon, the devil:

---

47   Song Bendizemos o teu nome (Blessed be your name)

Crushed it, oh Holy Virgin,	Esmagaste ó Virgem Santa,
All beautiful and immaculate,	Toda bela e imaculada,
The poisoned head	A cabeça envenenada
Of the deceptive dragon.	Do dragão enganador.
[...]	[...]

And finally, she is also titled «powerful advocate», who managed the trust of the world for being the refuge and the tab for the fair and, likewise, to the sinner who needs the consent of the Holy:

Powerful advocate,	Advogada poderosa,
The Universe trusts in you,	O Universo em ti confia,
Because thou art shelter and guide	Porque és tu refúgio e guia
For the righteous and the sinner	Para o justo e o pecador

About the above subject treated, the researcher Coyle (1999) notes that there is currently no coherent theology of Mary as a whole. She keeps being a religious symbol of enduring strength in the Christian imagination, a woman who has great powers, but she is also an ambiguous symbol, especially for women, because the passive virtues of submission, humility and docility were projected on her.

LITANY OF OUR LADY

It is in this hymn[48], a series of epithets that, as in other chants mentioned above, make references to the history of the passage of Mary on the Earth and the events that made her the "mother of us all", "the protective and the guide" of those who accepted her as Mother of God and intercessor between man and God:

---

[48] Song Ladainha de Nossa Senhora (Litany of Our Lady)

[...]	[...]
Virgin of the YES to the Word,	Virgem do SIM à Palavra,
Pray for us!	Rogai por nós!
Virgin of the love's risk	Virgem do risco do Amor,
Pray for us!	Rogai por nós!
Virgin of all joy,	Virgem de toda alegria,
Pray for us!	Rogai por nós!
[...]	[...]

The "Virgin of the YES to the Word" refers to the episode of the visit of the angel Gabriel to Mary, when she accepted the task of giving birth to Jesus. She accepted the request of God transmitted by the angel, risking her own life, "Virgin of Love's risk," according to the scriptures, she followed the precepts with great joy, "Virgin of all joy."

Similarly, it can highlight the following fragments that qualify the Holy as that one who did not deny the coming of Jesus and said "yes" to the angel Gabriel:

Blessed, for believing,	Bem-aventurada, porque acreditaste,
Handmaid of the Lord, servant of thy people,	Serva do Senhor, servidora do teu povo,
Saying yes to God, the Savior you gave birth	Dizendo sim a Deus, o Salvador geraste
And mankind saw the light of the new world.	E a humanidade viu a luz do mundo novo.
[...] [49]	[...]

God made you the most beautiful,	Deus Te fez a mais bela,
God made you the favourite	Deus Te fez predilecta
conceived without stain ...	concebida sem mancha...
You answered with love,	Respondeste em amor,
in Your "Yes savior"	no Teu "Sim salvador",
in Your "Yes trust."	no Teu "Sim confiança".
[...] [50]	[...]

---

49 50

---

49   Song Homenagem a Maria (Tribute to Mary)
50   Song Vamos ao teu altar (Let thy altar)

You did a long walk, To serve Isabel, To make thee a house of God, After your yes to Gabriel. [...] [51]	Fizeste longa caminhada, Para servir a Isabel, Fazendo-te de Deus morada, Após teu sim a Gabriel. [...]
I am the mother of pure love: my Redeemer son, That I followed from Bethlehem to the cross! Come, children, to me, I teach you to say "YES" and also follow the footsteps of Jesus! [...][52]	Sou a mãe do puro amor: o meu filho Redentor, Que segui desde Belém até a cruz! Venham, filhos, até mim, lhes ensino a dizer "SIM", e a seguir também os passos de Jesus! [...]

The hymn «Litany of Our Lady» also features the following epithets:

[...] Virgin of high mountains, Pray for us! Virgin of enthusiasm, Pray for us! Virgin of the walker brother, Pray for us! [...]	[...] Virgem das altas montanhas, Rogai por nós! Virgem do entusiasmo, Rogai por nós! Virgem do irmão caminheiro, Rogai por nós! [...]

It is possible to say that Mary receives the title of "The Virgin of the high mountains" because she is a "servant of God" and maybe even in the highest places in the higher mountains. That one who encourages her people to follow the divine precepts, "Virgin of enthusiasm", and to walk in search of a place to live, "Virgin of the walker brother."

It is also observed in the following excerpt, a Mary who takes care of helpless, «Virgin of the Helpless,» and looking for the children, watching the homes, «Virgin of every household», and also making use of observations for world, she seeks peace, «Virgin of peace to the world»:

---

51   Song Maria, mãe dos caminhantes (Mary, mother of walkers)
52   Song O que sente o teu coração. (What your heart feels)

Virgin of the Helpless, Pray for us! Virgin of all households, Pray for us! Virgin of peace to the world, Pray for us! [...]	Virgem dos desamparados, Rogai por nós! Virgem de todos os lares, Rogai por nós! Virgem da paz para o mundo, Rogai por nós! [...]

Thus, we turn to that Mary who looks for people who make charity, donations, «Virgin of hands that give themselves». The issue of love is also evident, «Virgin of fruitful love» and «Virgin of consecrated love,» and it is specified in her maternal feature:

Virgin of hands that give themselves, Pray for us! Virgin of fruitful love, Pray for us! Virgin of consecrated love, Pray for us! [...]	Virgem das mãos que se doam, Rogai por nós! Virgem do amor tão fecundo, Rogai por nós! Virgem do amor consagrado, Rogai por nós! [...]

THOU ART THE GLORY OF JERUSALEM (HAIL MARY)

Mary is called the "Jerusalem of glory," "joy of the people of God," "honor of mankind," "blessed one chosen by God" and "refuge of the people of God." In a single chant[53], the author has collected a significant amount of titles, which help in an acceptance of a Mary increasingly recognized for her qualities.

Also, the short prayer "Hail Mary", inserted at the end of each sentence, further transmits the attachment, and respect the poem's author has for the Holy. She is valued in all the ways and the qualities exhibited here are very

---

53   Thou Cântico Tu és a glória de Jerusalém (Ave Maria) (Art the glory of Jerusalem (Hail Mary))

important to the devotee who believes in the sanctity of Mary. The Holy is seen as that one who's "worthy of being worshiped":

Thou art the glory of Jerusalem! HAIL, MARY!
You are the joy of God's people! HAIL, MARY!
[...]

Tu és a glória de Jerusalém! AVE, MARIA!
És a alegria do povo de Deus! AVE, MARIA!
[...]

It is considered the "Glory of Jerusalem", the pride of sacred age for Arabs, Jews and Christians, Jerusalem, thanks to its symbolic power has been historically the scene of horrific wars and massacres between the followers of God, Jehovah and Allah. Mary is, in this chant, recognized as the "joy of God's people," the people of Jerusalem.

You are the honor of mankind! HAIL, MARY!
You are the blessed one chosen by God! HAIL, MARY!
[...]

Tu és a honra da humanidade! AVE, MARIA!
És a ditosa por Deus escolhida! AVE, MARIA!
[...]

Also she is indicated as the "honor of mankind." This title is very generalizing, but the author firmly believes that the Virgin is the splendor of each and every human inhabitant of our world. She is the fortunate chosen by God to take care and look at the men, freeing them from evil.

Of your hands wonders came to us! HAIL, MARY!
You are the refuge of God's people! HAIL, MARY!
[...]

Das tuas mãos nos vieram prodígios! AVE, MARIA!
És o refúgio do povo de Deus! AVE, MARIA!
[...]

This is how Mary is presented by both the Gospels as the liturgy and by the Christian art. In the Gospels, there is a reserved Mary of the Annunciation but also the exalted woman of the Magnificat. Moreover, the figure of the woman in the book of Genesis and Revelation, in which the Christian tradition sees the Mother of God, expresses this double face: a woman of extreme vulnerability, but also endowed with a decisively victorious power:

What you did pleased the Lord! HAIL, MARY! Blessed be thou by our all powerful God! HAIL, MARY! [...]	O que fizeste agradou ao Senhor! AVE, MARIA Bendita sejas por Deus poderoso! AVE, MARIA! [...]

Mary will always be praised for having spoken "yes" to the angel Gabriel, for having received with much love the request to conceive Jesus. She was and will be remembered by people, Catholics and devotees, which will acclaim her name:

People of Earth, praise to Mary! HAIL MARY! Eternally acclaim her name! HAIL MARY!	Povos da terra, louvai a Maria! AVE MARIA! Eternamente aclamai o seu nome! AVE MARIA!

QUEEN ANGEL

Here[54] also, as in other texts analyzed, there is the very rich qualifying treatments on stretches as proof of nostalgic devotion in the Mother of God. The term Angel becomes extremely significant because it strengthens the great beauty and perfection of the Virgin, still joining the substantive *Queen*, which refers to a sovereign wife of a kingdom, the two words making up evidence of the high esteem and appreciation that the Holy won:

---

54   Song Saudação das crianças a Maria SS (Greeting from the children to Mary SS)

Save! Queen Angel,	Salve! Angelica Rainha,
Mother of immortal beauty,	Mãe de belleza immortal,
Light that forwards the souls	Luz que as almas encaminha
And keep away and free from harm.	E afasta e livra do mal.
I hail you, Mary.	Eu vos saudo, ó Maria.
Mother that after Jesus	Mãe que depois de Jesus
You are the hope and joy	Sois a esperança e a alegria
That flash to the sinners.	Que aos peccadores reluz.
[...]	[...]

There is also the following epithets: "Mother of immortal beauty", "Light that forwards the souls and keep away and free from harm" and "mother". They are terms that denote the importance of Mary to the author and further classifications that helps to spread the attachment to Mary.

Poor, sad creatures	Pobres, tristes creaturas
Banished of the sky - who is,	Do ceu banidas – quem é,
In this valley of bitterness,	Neste valle de amarguras,
That shows us the light of faith?	Que nos mostra a luz da fé?
Hear us, Mother of clemency,	Ouvi-nos, Mãe de clemencia,
Our soul trusts you;	Nossa alma confia em vós;
And in the fights of existence	E nas luctas da existencia
Have mercy on us!	Compadecei-vos de nós!

In these excerpts, the presence of a nearby Mary of the "poor" and "sad creatures" is also noted; those ones who somehow had few opportunities to a more dignified and happier life.

Called the "Mother of Mercy", Mary is placed as a Holy truly protective and full of goodness. Thus, it appears that the author conveys through the chants, the trust that the souls of all those who needs it, who have struggles in their lives, have in Mary.

BENIGNANT

In the song "Keep us in the Heart (Look, Benignant)" as well as other songs analyzed in this work, Mary is called "benignant". Perhaps the scenes of the angel Gabriel's visitation and Cana are sources of inspiration for the development of poems that show Mary as a woman who is included in a social plan, of assistance, charity and human promotion.

Look benignant Virgin Mary Your people who trust in you What happy port of salvation Keep us always in your heart. [...]	Olhai benigna, Virgem Maria O vosso povo que em Vós confia Qual feliz porto de salvação Guardai-nos sempre em vosso Coração. [...]

In this passage, it is requested that Mary look for the people who trust her. There is an indication that the Holy is "happy port of salvation", so she really can, taking into account the above, keep "their children" in the heart; that is, she can protect them with all the "mother love ".

It checks up such processes of love, dedication and comfort of Mary to «her children» in sections listed below:

-The one who sustains, comforts and guides:

Oh Mary, Mother that saves the
mortal,
Sustain me and guide me to the
homeland
heavenly
[...]⁵⁵

Ó Maria, ó Mãe pia, salvadora do
mortal,
Amparai-me e guiai-me para a pátria
celestial.
[...]

Uma entre todas foi a escolhida:

One among all was chosen:
it was you, Mary, preferred servant,
Mother of my Lord,
Mother of my Savior!
Mary, full of grace and consolation,
come walk with your people.
Our mother and always you will be!
[...]⁵⁶

foste tu, Maria, serva preferida,
Mãe do meu Senhor,
Mãe do meu Salvador!
Maria, cheia de graça e consolo,
venha caminhar com teu povo.
Nossa mãe e sempre serás!
[...]

55 56

-That one who saves in times of difficulties:

Sweet Heart of Mary,
Be our salvation,

Doce coração de Maria,
Sêde nossa salvação,

When body disease
Cause us serious affliction
When Satan Cursed
Comes to us with the temptation,
When the evil doubts
Disturb our heart

Quando corporal doença
Nos cuasar grave afficção,
Quando de Satan Maldito
Nos vier a tentação,
Quando a duvida maligna
Nos turbar o coração

When in the dreadful death
We ask for protection
And when we get to the judgment
We will fear the condemnation⁵⁷.

Quando na medonha morte
Vos pedir-mos protecção,
Ao chegar-mos ao juízo
Temendo a condemnação

57

---

55   Song Salvadora do mortal (Savior of the mortal one)
56   Song Uma entre todas (One among all)
57   Song Doce coração de Maria (Sweet heart of Mary)

-The mediatrix who appears to the poor and pilgrims:

[...]
Mary, Mediatrix of all graces,
You are our Intercessory with your Son!
Begs the Church: that it be holy:
We want to see and love Jesus!
Shows us the face of the Eternal who is born,
[...]
Mary, Appeared to the poor, small,
Being humble made you servant Queen!
Crown it offers to you from your people, singing and praying,
Star of Evangelization you are!
Your holiness, the new humanity,
Make us all citizens of heaven! [58]

[...]
Maria, Medianeira de todas as graças,
És nossa Intercessora junto ao Filho teu!
Suplica pela Igreja: que santa ela seja:
Ver e amar nós queremos Jesus!
Mostra-nos a face que do Eterno nasce,
[...]
Maria, Aparecida aos pobres, pequenos,
O ser humilde serva rainha te fez!
Coroa te oferece teu povo, em canto e prece,
Estrela és da Evangelização!
Tua santidade, nova humanidade,
Faça de nós todos do céu cidadãos!

58

---

58 Song Maria Imaculada (Mary Immaculate)

- That one who is Lady of the pilgrims:

Sister pilgrim of all the poor people
prophetess woman of freed poor ones.
With all those who follow Christ,
to thee we call mother.
[...][59]

Holy Mary, Oh Virgin of hope
And the poor's mother, Lady of
pilgrims.
The People you guide with joy, until
we find
the light: your Jesus! Amen.
Oh Virgin of Hope, the continent
awakens,
To bright the new dawn.
[...][60]

Irmã peregrina de todos os pobres
mulher profetisa dos pobres libertos.
Com todos aqueles que seguem a
Cristo,
a ti nós chamamos de mãe.
[...]

Santa Maria, ó Virgem da esperança
E mãe dos pobres, Senhora dos
peregrinos.
O povo guia na alegria, até
encontrarmos
a luz: teu Jesus! Amém.
Ó Virgem da esperança, o continente
desperta,
Ao brilho da nova aurora.

The following epithets found in the last excerpt: "Holy Mary", "Virgin of hope", "the poor's mother," "Lady of pilgrims" and "Virgin of Hope", shows us a Mary who was exiled in Egypt in order to save her son Jesus Christ, lived the sad experience of several exiled migrants who over the centuries, escaped from hunger and violence, as well as political and religious persecution.

Such persecution that led Mary and Joseph to seek a safe haven for the child, the one who "was chosen" to be the "Savior." Jesus Christ was generated in a political framework of colonial domination, signaled by the name of Augustus Caezar, and also in the context of a census, political instrument of economic exploitation: the extraction of the head tax (BOFF, C., 2006).

Following this exposure, it is observed that in the above-mentioned sections there are several titles and phrases that qualify Mary as "Mother of the pilgrims." Just as she had to move very often in order to protect the Son Jesus Christ, many people in Brazil and in several other places in the world, had to abandon their homes in search of a better space, in search of land and that

---

59   Song Irmã peregrina de todos os pobres (Sister pilgrim of all the poor)
60   Song Cântico Mãe da América Latina (Mother of Latin America)

mainly went on pilgrimage to places considered holy: Aparecida do Norte (Brazil), Bethlehem, Nazareth, Jerusalem, St. Peter's Basilica, Sanctuary of Fatima, Lourdes, Medjugorje, Basilica of Guadalupe and others.

On this issue, the Archbishop Murilo Sebastião Krieger says that,

> The number of pilgrims in large and small Marian shrines is growing in various parts of the world. Pilgrim (from 'peragrare': go 'per agros ", outside the city, in the countryside) is the one that goes away, that makes a trip to a certain place, to remain there for some time. In the nineteenth century, it grew considerably the pilgrimages to Marian shrines, especially since the apparitions of Lourdes (1858). The pilgrim is attracted by Mary; they know she will lead them to Christ, who, in turn, will lead to the Father. 'It repeated the path of incarnation: as the Word came among men through the mediation and the participation of Mary, the faithful also come close to Christ by the same way: the active motherhood of Mary. [...] Mary is not indifferent to the path of the Church and of Christ's disciples, having traveled the path before us [...], she is not only an example, but [...] she is also guide and help on the way '(ROSSO 1955, p. 1032). (Krieger, 2005, p. 22).

The pilgrims are very noticeable among Catholic. Each commemorative day of some saint or patron of certain areas, one can see a different movement of romeiros and pilgrims from various parts of Brazil. The pilgrims follow from Aparecida do Norte (Our Lady of Aparecida) to Juazeiro do Norte, Ceará (Father Cicero).

In romarias (kind of pilgrimage in Brazil), there is a constant worship of Mary, the romeiros gather to sing in one voice the words that glorify the name of the Holy; the moments of the Virgin's life are remembered and repeated along the path made by the pilgrims:

100

Behold, oh Mary, romeiros	Eis aqui, ó Maria, romeiros
who is coming today to be near you	Que vêm hoje pr'a junto de vós
Chanting your name, trembling,	Vosso nome entoando, fremente,
In unison voice concerts. [61]	Em concertos de uníssona voz.

Following there is an examination of the chant "Our Lady (dear mother)" in order to present some more elements related to the pilgrimage to the Marian chants:

Our Lady; oh, dear mother!	Nossa Senhora; oh, mãe querida!
Look to us, give me your hand	Olhai por nós, me dê a sua mão
Our Lady; oh, dear mother!	Nossa Senhora; oh, mãe querida!
Pray for us, guard my heart	Rogai por nós, guarda meu coração
Oh, holy virgin, cover with your mantle this pilgrim!	Oh, virgem santa, cubra com seu manto esse peregrino!
Oh, Divine Mother, come dry our tears and lead the way!	Oh, mãe divina, vem secar o pranto e mostrar o caminho!
I went on foot to the holy church	
May God protect our prayer!	Eu fui a pé até a santa igreja
Asking for peace, love, health, well ...	Que Deus proteja nossa oração!
Listen to this song	Pedindo paz, amor, saúde, enfim...
[...]	Escute essa canção
	[...]

In this excerpt, it's investigated, above all, how the pilgrims are remembered and resort to the protection of Mary. "Our Lady" must be with the romeiros so the hike can take place effectively.

Also called on the fragment "dear mother", "holy virgin", "Divine Mother," Mary is seen as one that gives courage, faith and wisdom so that the people can face the events that happen in life. Mary is the Holy who guards, looks, illuminates the hearts and takes care of the people who bends their knees and makes prayers:

---

61   Song Na Basílica. (In the Basilica)

Give me courage, faith, wisdom To face the hardships of life Always guard me on thee Our Lady; oh, dear mother!	Me dê coragem, fé, sabedoria Pra encarar as agruras da vida Me guardai sempre em ti Nossa Senhora; oh, mãe querida!
Our Lady, look for us in this worldwide Take care of these people now who makes a kneeling prayer Our Lady; oh, holy virgin, bless this child! With your bright enlighten the way Where our hearts are going.	Nossa Senhora, olhai por nós por esse mundo afora Toma de conta desse povo agora Que de joelhos faz uma oração Nossa Senhora; oh, virgem santa, abençoa esse filho! Com sua luz iluminai o trilho Por onde anda o nosso coração.

LADY APARECIDA

Going back to the initial element of the story of Mary in Brazil, it identifies the lady who "appeared", the "Lady of Aparecida," the "chief guardian" of the people. These terms are well known, especially among Catholic. Great importance has been given to the meaning of "Lady Aparecida" for Brazil, being the 12th of October a national holiday dedicated to her:

[...] Oh Lady of Aparecida! Our main guardian, Always protect our lives Freeing us from all evil [...][62]	[...] Ó Senhora de Aparecida! Nossa guardiã principal, Proteja sempre nossa vida Livrando-nos de todo mal [...]

The term "Mother of God and ours" presents a Mary who, besides being the mother of the «Savior «, is also mother of the people, indicating a closer relationship with the Holy who divides her maternal role not only with Jesus but also with the devotees:

---

[62]   Song Negra Senhora Aparecida (Black Lady Aparecida).

Long live the Mother of God and ours,	Viva a mãe de Deus e nossa,
Conceived without sin!	Sem pecado concebida!
Long live the immaculate virgin,	Viva a virgem imaculada,
Oh Lady of Aparecida.	Ó Senhora Aparecida.
[...][63]	[...]

The following extract is understandable as Mary associated with each pilgrim, both in "passion" as her joys. The Holy reveals herself as a caring woman and present in each situation, having then full attention of the devotees:

Here there are your devotees,	Aqui estão vossos devotos,
Full of faith,	Cheios de fé incendida,
Of comfort and hope.	De confôrto e de esperança.
Oh Lady Aparecida!	Ò Senhora Aparecida!
Hear our prayers ...	Nossos rogos escutai...
Our voice be answered!	Nossa voz seja atendida!
Of the deeper place of our soul we ask,	Do imo d'alma vos pedimos,
Oh Lady Aparecida!	Ó Senhora Aparecida!
	No Calvário junto à Cruz
On Calvary beneath the Cross	Com a alma de dor ferida,
With the soul of wound pain,	Jesus vos fez nossa Mãe,
Jesus made you our Mother,	Ó Senhora Aparecida!
Oh Lady Aparecida!	[...]
[...][64]	

Mary is proclaimed and chanted. The author of the poem makes a rich mention of the Mother of God, calling her the "Holy Virgin", "beautiful Virgin," "loving Mother", "Dear Mother" and "Patroness of Brazil", the one who was chosen by God to help men on earth:

---

63   Song Viva a mãe de Deus e Nossa (Long live the Mother of God and Our)
64   Ibid.

Holy Virgin, beautiful virgin,	Virgem Santa, Virgem bela,
Loving Mother, dear Mother,	Mãe amável, Mãe querida,
Support us, help us,	Amparai-nos, socorrei-nos,
Oh Lady Aparecida!	Ó Senhora Aparecida!
Aiming big purposes	Visando altos desígnios
You have been chosen by God	Fostes por Deus escolhida
Patroness of Brazil,	Padroeira do Brasil,
Oh Lady Aparecida!	Ó Senhora Aparecida!
[...]	[...]

Most of the texts made in honor of Mary show that she fulfilled the role assigned by God. Inspired by the power of God, Mary is contemplated and admired by many devotees. She is presented in a large number of verses, as the protector and patron of the Catholic Church, which protects the homeland, bolsters the Clergy, watches over the families, the needy children and the Brazilian people:

Who proclaimed you	Quem assim vos proclamou
Complied with the order received,	Cumpriu ordem recebida,
Inspired by Heaven,	Inspirado pelo Céu,
Oh Lady Aparecida!	Ó Senhora Aparecida!
Protect the Holy Church,	Protegei a Santa Igreja,
Loving mother and compassionate,	Mãe terna e compadecida,
Protect our Motherland,	Protegei a nossa Pátria,
Oh Lady Aparecida!	Ó Senhora aparecida!
Support all the clergy,	Amparai a todo o Clero,
In its earthly read,	Em sua terrena lida,
For the sake of sinners,	Para bem dos pecadores,
Oh Lady Aparecida!	Ó Senhora Aparecida!
Watch over our families,	Velai por nossas famílias,
Needy children,	Pela infância desvalida,
The Brazilian people	Pelo povo brasileiro
Oh Lady Aparecida!	Ó Senhora Aparecida!
[...]	[...]

With the same sense it can be checked in the following excerpt, passages that show the role of Mary in Brazil, indicating the many purposes of the Brazilian devout people:

Holy Mother Mary, at this crossing,
Cover us with your indigo mantle.
Guard our life, Mother Aparecida,
Patron saint of Brazil.
Hail Mary, Hail Mary.
[...] [65]

Santa Mãe Maria, nessa travessia,
Cubra-nos teu manto cor de anil.
Guarda nossa vida, Mãe Aparecida,
Santa padroeira do Brasil.
Ave Maria, Ave Maria.
[...]

It is noted the "Holy Mother Mary" playing the role of protector, which helps in "crossing", covering people with the blue mantle. The "Mother Aparecida" and "patron saint of Brazil" was chosen to take care of life of the people and pilgrims who walk in search of a desire, whether it is to have their own home or to get at the place where there's the image of the desired saint.

THE QUEEN OF BRAZIL

Mary is considered "Queen of Brazil", chosen to represent the celestial nobility in a country that expresses a sincere attachment to her, it's no wonder she has been selected to be the patron saint of Brazil.

The devotion to Mary in Latin America, particularly in Brazil, shows the fascination that the figure of the Holy exercises in the popular imagination. In this sense, the epithet "Queen of Brazil", used by the author of the poem[66] says as the Mother of Jesus is an eminent figure in the country. In the West, the cultural representation of Mary suffered a similar trend to the East: She was servant and became a Queen (SCHREINER,1996).

In the Gospel there are basis for the royal understanding of the Virgin: she is fundamentally the «Messiah-King›s Mother», so it is a royalty that is primarily

---

65   Song Santa Mãe Maria (Holy Mother Mary)
66   Song Rainha do Brasil (Queen of Brazil)

spiritual, which the idea of political power is a little more spaced, although not totally excluded:

> [...] The idea of Mary Queen was a main theme in the artistic representations of the environments of nobility. It's common figuring scenes in which Mary appears, majestic, on the throne as Sovereign. Thus, for example, the scene of the visit of the Magi: they are the kings of the whole earth that honor the King of the world, who appears however, sitting in the Queen Mother's lap. Another scene that appears frequently is the Assumption of Mary in glory and her coronation in heaven. It clearly notes that such representations have everything to do with the vision of the emerging aristocracies, whether the kings of the new converts people, whether of imperial dynasties (BOFF, C., 2006, p. 162).

This author still continues saying:

> ...] the level of the people in general, the figure of the Holy Virgin as Queen and Lady radiated spiritual strength, with strong existential projections. For medieval people, the heavenly Queen exercised with Christ a mercy function: as the defender of the weak one and the intercessor of the sinner. She is the 'Queen and Mother of Mercy', the 'Reconciler', the "Gentle Woman'. She is invoked as *sweetest Domina*, as *Advocatrix, Refugium, Solatium, Precatrix, Mediatrix*. She has "bowels of mercy" because in them she carried God. (BOFF, C., 2006, p. 163).

This image of Mary represented in the environments of nobility, sitting on the throne, was without doubt, taken into account by the author of the song, that by using the term of *Queen of Brazil* already checks the authority offered to

Mary. The author then says that the Nazarene is a noble and high woman of the Brazilian nation, a saint who was chosen among other saints to represent this place so much need of "royalty" divine, which is found in her:

Virgin Mother Aparecida,	Virgem Mãe Aparecida,
You are the Brazilian homeland,	És da Pátria Brasileira,
Noble and exalted patroness,	Nobre e excelsa Padroeira,
The Queen of Brazil	A Rainha do Brasil
[...]	[...]

Similarly, there is in the following stretch that many of the riches of Brazil are exposed as properties of Mary, which can be classified in this situation as "Peacemaker", as the quoted made by Clodovis Boff (2006). The song says that Mary is the "owner" of nature, green meadows, dense forests, valleys, mountains, that means that she might just even be considered the "Queen of Brazil"; because only with that title someone could have such dominion over all the natural elements in Brazil:

Our country devotes you	Nossa Pátria te consagra
All that dwell therein,	Tudo quanto nela habita,
All is yours, Oh Blessed Mother,	Tudo é teu, ó Mãe Bendita,
In this land of Brazil.	Nesta terra do Brasil.
Green meadows, dense forests,	Verdes prados, densas matas,
All is yours on our earth,	Tudo é teu em nossa Terra,
Your valley, your saw,	Teu o vale, tua a serra,
Also is yours the indigo sky .	Teu também o céu de anil.
[...]	[...]

Mary is receiving also the title of «Queen of the World», it was not seen in all the chants analyzed in this work, but it is an element that expresses social relevance that, according to the Magisterium, the figure of the Virgin continues to have in the context of the modern world and its complex problem.

For this, it was crucial the proclamation of Mary's feast "Queen of the World", through the work of Pius XII, the Marian year 1954 through the encyclical *Ad coeli reign* on November 11 of that year. That title had solid biblical foundations, patristic and liturgical (BOFF, C., 2006).

There is also, in the following hymns, epithets rather correlated to the above, emphasizing the image of Mary centered in Brazil and in the diaspora, a Mary brunette, colored skin, with African and also indigenous traits.

| Brazil of Mary is kingdom and nation,
Brazil be the throne of her heart.

Sing Brazilians sing with fervor:
Reign, Mary, your Heart! [67] | Brasil de Maria é reino e nação,
Brasil seja o trono do seu Coração.

Cantai, brasileiros, cantai com fervor:
Que reine, Maria, o teu Coração! |

67

In the "Brazil of Mary" song, the composer expresses concern over the integrity of the Brazilian nation, presenting Mary as the "head of state" or "Empress of the Brazilian people"; she is symbolically invited to reign in the hearts of the people.

In this other Marian text there is the «Queen of Brazil» being called «Brunette Saint», which is well-connected to the people of indigenous descent, who went through various acculturation processes and simultaneously suffered the loss of material basis (the earth), necessary for the maintenance of its social model:

| [...]
Brunette Saint, I am a Brazilian Indigenous, the first people of this land.
We were thousands, today we are nothing,
In the earth I live for opinion.
If you allow me a confession:
The land is mine and I will not give up! [68] | [...]
Santa morena sou um brasileiro Índio, primeiro povo deste chão.
Fomos milhares, hoje somos nada,
Na terra vivo por opinião.
Se me permitem uma confissão:
A terra é minha e eu não abro mão! |

68

---

67   Song Brasil de Maria (Brazil of Mary)
68   Song Aparecida Santuário Brasileiro (Aparecida Brazilian Sanctuary)

Figure: Photograph of a T-shirt of Song Liberation Festival - (Festival da Canção Libertadora, in portuguese) FECALE - Presidente Prudente, SP, Brazil.

About what was exposed, the theologian Clodovis Boff (2006) says that African slaves brought to Brazil learned, among other devotions, to honor Mary. The recitation of the Rosary was taught to african slaves and it was allowed to organize their brotherhoods, such as Our Lady of the Rosary of the Black People[69]. As seen by the sermons of Father Vieira[70] on the Rosary preached to slaves, it was primarily a function of evangelization and, secondly, a consolidation and even resignation in the face of their condition of servant. The researcher emphasized that

> the devotion to Our Lady of Mercy, developed, especially among the **colored slaves**, especially in gold villages: Diamantina, São João del Rei, Mariana, Sabará, where several churches dedicated to her won an assistance character and social protection , leading the slaves to buy their freedom. And it's natural because it was about the 'liberator of the captives' often represented with just the hands squashed on shackles. The colored people of Diamantina always thought it was Our Lady of Mercy who inspired the Princess Isabel to sign the abolition. (BOFF, C., 2006, p. 230, emphasis added).

From this perspective, the epithet «Brunette Saint» is very well exposed by the author of the poem, because it has in its content the hardships suffered by enslaved blacks, who, to mitigate the sufferings, needed to worship a patron saint, confessing to «Our Lady of Aparecida» their idols (heroes) and insurrectionary desires:

---

69   Known as Our Lady of the Rosary of Black Men, the brotherhood is still in full exercise in the following Brazilian states: São Paulo, Rio de Janeiro, Minas Gerais, Rio Grande do Norte, Rio Grande do Sul and Bahia.
70   According to the researcher Valerio Alberton (1994), among the 30 sermons of the Rosary, by Father Vieira, three are directed to colored people: Sermons XIV, XX and XXVII.

Brunette Saint, I am a Brazilian
BLACK, slave of domination.
Blood of the race on the sea was
released
Zumbi reborn of my prayer.
If you allow me a confession:
New "Quilombos" will come soon!
Brunette Saint, I am FOREIGN
It said foreign but why?
My parents came from another
flag.
From north to south, I did grow the
Nation
If you allow me a confession:
We are seed, powder of the same
ground![71]
[...]

Santa morena sou um brasileiro
NEGRO, escravo da dominação.
Sangue da raça, no mar foi lançado
Zumbi renasce da minha oração.
Se me permite uma confissão:
Novos "Quilombos" logo surgirão!
Santa morena sou ESTRANGEIRO
Dito estrangeiro mas porque razão?
Meus pais vieram de outra bandeira.
De norte a sul, fiz crescer a Nação
Se me permite uma confissão:
Somos semente, pó do mesmo chão!
[...]

Following the same subject, it shows on the hymn "Colored Mother of heaven" meanings related to the previous discussion:

Colored Mother of heaven
Lady of Latin America
your look and charity are so divine,
of color equal to the color of many
races,
Virgin so serene, Lady of these people
so suffered,
Patroness of small and oppressed
ones,
pour upon us your graces.
[...][72]

Mãe do céu morena
Senhora da América Latina
de olhar e caridade tão divina,
de cor igual à cor de tantas raças,
Virgem tão serena, Senhora desses
povos tão sofridos,
Patrona dos pequenos e oprimidos,
derrama sobre nós as tuas graças.
[...]

72

---

71   Song Aparecida Santuário brasileiro (Aparecida Brazilian Sanctuary)
72   Song Mãe do céu morena (Colored Mother of heaven)

Mary is described as a " Colored Mother of heaven", "Lady of Latin America", "Virgin so serene","Lady of these people so suffered" and "patron of small and oppressed ones." They are terms that indicate a saint dedicated to the "suffering people" who had their land taken, the oppressed and enslaved by forced migration from North to South that produce the nation's wealth without being able to take any advantage.

In this sense, it can say that Our Lady of Guadalupe is a figure that fits perfectly into the lives of these suffered people, since she exerted a significant influence of liberating character. The devotion to this Saint was widespread at the time when Brazil passed under a Spanish domain (1580-1640). It can be seen in the sections following the signs of Mary liberator:

People of America! Suffering people, where hope insists in germinate! People of America! What joy! There are so many races, voices singing!

Blacks and whites, Indigenous, mestizos, of all God is Father! Only one faith, only one Savior! World Evangelize!

Come, Behold! And Declare! [...]

Oh Mother of America! Of Guadalupe, of Aparecida and many more names! Virgin Mary, Mother of these people, behold your children, whom you love so much! [73]

Povos d'América! Gente sofrida, onde a esperança insiste em germinar! Povos d'América! Quanta alegria! São tantas raças, vozes a cantar!

Negros e brancos, índios, mestiços, de todos Deus é pai! Uma só fé, um só Salvador! O mundo evangelizai!

Vinde, Vede! E Anunciai! [...]

Ó Mãe d'América! De Guadalupe, de Aparecida e tantos nomes mais! Virgem Maria, Mãe destes povos, eis vossos filhos, a quem tanto amais!

73

73   Song Povos da América – Vinde, vede e anunciai! (America Peoples - Come, see and tell!)

The epithets "Mother of America", "of Guadalupe", "Aparecida" and "Mother of these people" are elements that relate Mary worshiped in Brazil with the other "Marys" of different attributes, but having the same meaning: the liberation of the poor and humble ones[74] and people considered inferior[75].

It is observed in this other fragment, the same Saint liberator of the wrong ones, qualified here as «Mary of Liberation» and «dear mother of Latin American»; Mary›s figure gets, with all authority, the reward of Latin people›s representative :

Partner with thy people, Mary of Liberation	Companheira com teu povo, Maria da Libertação
From the manger to the cross, your life marked our ground.	Do presépio até a cruz, tua vida marcou nosso chão.
Meet, oh Latin American darling mother, the screaming of	Atende, ó mãe querida Latino-Americana, o grito do
thy people. That Call for justice and cry[76]!	teu povo. Que pede justiça e clama!

According to the words of the researcher Clodovis Boff (1995), this "Colored Mary" is an image with which undoubtedly slaves identified themselves as well as the oppressed ones in general. The author also says that, although it was manipulated according to the *status quo*, her original message is essentially liberating.

Following the concept of Mary who freed the people, it shows the Marian text below, facing the biblical hymn *Magnificat[77]*, a chant made by Mary to greet her cousin Elizabeth.

---

74   The Virgin was humble and established a strong contact with those who were also considered lowly (AUTRAN, 2001).

75   In biblical language, the poor, humble and lower are clear references to Israel, often in conditions of domination, oppression and distress (HORSLEY, 1989).

76   Song Maria da Libertação (Our Lady of Liberation)

77   Luke (1, 46:56).

The Magnificat is a kind of "automaryology"[78], being the first result of the Mother of Jesus meditation around elements that involved her intimately (Luke, 2:19). It is seen that in such events Mary sees the arrival of the messianic liberation.

Thus, based on the Canticle of Mary, the hymn *"Mary sang the Magnificat"* makes a mention of the words in the music left by Mary, which reinforces the issue of the need for food that a portion of the Brazilian people has:

<table>
<tr><td>

Mary sang the Magnificat
and with her we will sing it.
Bread and Life is the scream of a Brazil
that from north to south joined
to eliminate the hunger.
[...]

</td><td>

Maria o Magnificat cantou
e com ela também nós vamos cantar.
Pão e vida é o brado de um Brasil
que de norte a sul se uniu
para a fome eliminar.
[...]

</td></tr>
</table>

The excerpts from the last chant invigorate, in a way, the liberating character of Mary. There is here a junction between the colored and indigenous Holy, dedicated to the poor and pilgrims that were portrayed throughout this research. It also unites in one "network", the liberty proposals proclaimed to the image of the Virgin and representations of devotees who are imbued to intervene directly in the context of social injustices:

<table>
<tr><td>

Aparecida is the Fisherman's mother,
the mother of the Savior,
the mother of us all.

Mary sang the Magnificat
and with her we will sing it,
protecting and defending our brother
that deserves fish and bread
to satiate his hunger

</td><td>

Aparecida é a mãe do pescador, é a mãe do Salvador,
é a mãe de todos nós.

Maria o magnificat cantou
e com ela também nós vamos cantar,
protegendo e defendendo nosso irmão
que merece peixe e pão
pra sua fome saciar

</td></tr>
</table>

---

78   A term used by Boff, C. (2006)

The main element of this hymn as the one of the Magnificat in the gospel can be summarized, from the social point of view, in the following factors: poverty, domination, oppression, worries and finally, the waiting for release of the part of belonging people to the "land", that means that " they were harassed and scattered, like sheep without a shepherd" (Matthew, 9:36):

[...]	[...]
Mary sang the Magnificat	Maria o magnificat cantou
and with her we will sing it,	e com ela também nós vamos cantar,
begging for suffering people	implorando pelo povo sofredor
that for lack of love	que por falta de amor
they have nothing to eat.[79]	não tem nada para comer.
[...]	[...]

Mary was chosen by the Evangelist Luke to sing the hymn (Song of the Virgin), which has become a paradigm of the Christian religious doctrine focused on liberating character. "That one who begs for suffering people, who has nothing to eat due to lack of love" is identified and beloved in all Marian hymns that here we set out to examine.

Faced with so many artists who were inspired by the Magnificat to produce works aimed at the "magnitude" of Mary, it would emphasize the tone of sublime exaltation to the chant of Nazareth woman, ornate by the speaker St. Tomás de Vilanova in the following text:

> Mary did not speak but rarely. But she was compelled to sing with sonorous voice, both the Spirit of God intoxicated her with his inspiration. Oh excessive effusion of divine emotion! Oh immense jolt of the heart! It was never heard a similar singing since the world began. That's the reason that the Magnificat is called the Song of Songs. As David, with his arpeggios, keep the spirit that tormented Saul away, thus by Mary chords, the devil is expelled ... Oh wonderful hymn! Jesus Christ said from the inside and the Virgin sings from the outside. The object of this song is so high that no language comes

---

79   Song Maria o Magnificat cantou (Mary sang the Magnificat)

to play its sublimity. Mary does not claim the victory of famous conquerors [...] She sings greater wonders, celebrates highest mysteries and recognizes magnificent benefits. She gives thanks not only for a prophet son, but the God and Lord of the prophets. She sings the Creator who carries in her womb the Word made flesh, the merciful bowels of divine goodness, **the big lowered ones, the small exalted ones, the fortified poor ones,** the infinite power of love, the world's repair, the defeat of the Devil, the destruction of sin. Here they are the noble themes she sings. Sappho, by chance, did flow more melodious songs? Did the lira of that poet release one day softest sounds? The admirable style corresponds to the height of the mystery. A fascinating grace reigns throughout the whole song. Silence, muses of all ages! Close in the silence the furious syllables! Hide the poetry Silence the sweet mermaid! And the nightingale henceforth ceases its twittering! Silence, Silence, harmonious praises of men and birds! The real harp resonates, the Virgin Mother of God sings! Oh most beautiful of all women, make us hear your voice, because your voice is so sweet and your face, infinitely beautiful! (AUGSBURG, 1957 cited BOFF, C., 2006, p. 335-336, emphasis added).

So we close this cycle. The *Magnificat* was sang by Mary and the extent of this hymn the man undertook to do in order to not silence the voice of what has become the "great mother" of all time, who circulated in medieval palaces and entered as a generous inspiration act the paths of the various Marian composers of our time, who turn their words new songs of praise.

4. Inspiring Women

The set of hymns explored in this book presents a lot of information about the life of Mary and the songs she inspired, trying to show the epithets present in these texts.

The lack of more historical information about Mary is offset by the quality and the titles that the texts presented and brought in this work. There is also this exhibition that sheds light on it, because the songs have tried, in one way or another, to elucidate the liberating role of this woman, which has a special meaning in the lives of many Christians.

For Leonardo Boff (1990), for example, without Mary it would miss something in the history of all men, in that we would be deprived of the collaboration and presence of women that make up the "other half of the human beings." The reports that we find about the Virgin Mary are always fruitful, that can be leveraged to clarify and fit to be disclosed.

The hundreds of description treatments we had the opportunity to meet, through Marian texts, are characteristics that if it had not been made public and popular through the Marian songs we would not have had the opportunity to meet and study them.

There are many probabilities to find a song in honor of Mary, because she has a prominent place in the prayer language of the Christian life: prayers, chants, novenas, poems and devotions. Among the prayers we can mention the following: the Rosary, the Hail Mary, the Angel of the Lord, the Hail Holy Queen, the Litany of Our Lady, the Litany of the Blessed Virgin Mary, the small craft of the Madonna and the Seven Dolors of Mary; moreover, the months of May, September and October are especially consecrated to Mary; a weekly worship which is dedicated to the Saturday; songs and celebrations of the Virgin; and there is also the perpetual worship that are consecrated by the Marian Associations (Orders, Fellowships, Youth Associations).

The study, conducted primarily through the story of Mary and the epithets found in fifty songs, took as a starting point the selection of hymns, which are located in several copies of song books; they can also be found in Catholic Churches from the Northern to Southern Brazil and in other places meant to disclose the Marian topic work. In almost all Marian contemporary chants surveyed, it was possible to find a kind of qualifying term. From them, the less visible but not less important, we can find those with a simple "title", already seen in other situations, for example, using the terms "mother", "our mother," "Mother of God and ours" and "Hail Mary" . In a few cases, we find the use of the name "Mary", that does not fit here as a Holy qualifying, since it is her name.

Surveying the various titles that have been entrusted to Mary, it was possible to ascertain that a large number of them is facing the idea of a holy liberator, whose primary function is to care for the poor ones and free them from sin and despair. Thus, it was concluded that the many hymns disseminated among the people deal with recurring themes that value Mary. The Holy is an inspiration in the reality lived in Brazil for many people seeking spiritual freedom, comfort, hope, inspiration and other types of aid.

It can be seen that the inventive faculty of popular pity is oriented toward Mary, as these songs are. The Marian pity is one of the most important aspects of contemporary Catholic devotion - from the cult of the Virgin Mary are expected the most eminent benefits- whether in life, in death and after death. The songs disclose the graces of the "Shining Star" and the epithets reviewed here try to confirm them.

Therefore, the study of these Marian songs, based on epithets, brought a lot of information that make it possible to raise awareness of the importance of this religious figure who is Mary for the Brazilian culture, knowing that there are studies dealing with the subject, but hardly take as their starting point the question of the present titles in the Marian songs. In addition, bringing to the scientific community a seemingly new approach on studies related to the qualifying terms, elements not so explored in academia.

REFERENCES

AGOSTINHO (Santo). A Virgem Maria: cem textos marianos com comentários. São Paulo: Paulus, 1996.

ALBERTON, Valério. O Rosário de Vieira. São Paulo: Loyola, 1994.

AUGRAS, Monique. Todos os santos são bem-vindos. Rio de Janeiro: Pallas, 2005.

AUTRAN, Aleixo Maria. A humilde Virgem Maria. São Paulo: Editora FTD, 2001.

AZEVEDO, Manuel Quitério. O culto a Maria no Brasil: história e teologia. Aparecida, SP: Editora Santuário/Academia Marial, 2001.

AZZI, Riolando. A espiritualidade popular no Brasil: um enfoque histórico. Revista Grande Sinal, Petrópolis, Vozes, ano XLVII, 1994.

BEINERT, Wolfgang (Org.). O culto a Maria hoje. São Paulo: Paulinas, 1979.

BERCEO,Gonçalo. Milagros de Nuestra Señora. 6. ed. Madri: Espasa-Calpe, 1964.

BOFF, Clodovis Maria. Maria na cultura brasileira. Aparecida, Iemanjá, N. S. da libertação. Petrópolis: Vozes, 1995.

_____. Mariologia social: o significado da Virgem para a sociedade. São Paulo: Paulus, 2006.

BOFF, Leonardo. A Ave-Maria: o feminino e o Espírito Santo. Petrópolis: Vozes, 1990.

BOFF, Leonardo; BOFF, Clodovis. Como fazer Teologia da Libertação. Petrópolis: Vozes, 1985.

CHAUÍ, Marilena. Conformismo e resistência: aspectos da cultura popular no Brasil. São Paulo: Brasiliense, 1989.

COYLE, Khatleen. Maria na tradição cristã: a partir de uma perspectiva contemporânea. São Paulo: Paulus, 1999.

DICIONÁRIO AURÉLIO. O minidicionário da Língua Portuguesa: século XXI. Rio de Janeiro: Editora Nova Fronteira, 2001.

DURAND, Gilbert. As estruturas antropológicas do imaginário. São Paulo: Martins Fontes, 1997.

DURKHEIM, Emile. As formas elementares de vida religiosa. São Paulo: Paulus, 1998.

ELIADE, Mircea. O sagrado e o profano: a essência das religiões. Lisboa: Livros do Brasil, 1983.

FRANÇA, Maria Cecília. Pequenos Centros Paulistas de Função Religiosa. 1972. Tese (Doutorado) – Faculdade de Filosofia, Letras e Ciências Humanas, Universidade de São Paulo, São Paulo, 1972.

GONZÁLEZ, Antônio. De Maria conquistadora a Maria libertadora: Mariologia popular latino-americana. São Paulo: Loyola, 1992.

HOONAERT, Eduardo. A história do catolicismo no Brasil. Petrópolis: Vozes, 1979.

HOUAISS, Antônio. Dicionário Houaiss da Língua Portuguesa. Rio de Janeiro: Editora Objetiva, 2001.

KOLLING, Miria Therezinha; BORTOLINI, José. Nas asas do amor. São Paulo: Paulus, 2003.

KRAMER, Sonia. Por entre as pedras: arma e sonho na escola. São Paulo: Ática 1993.

KRIEGER, Murilo. Maria na piedade popular. São Paulo: Paulus, 2005.

LARRAÑAGA, Inácio. O silêncio de Maria. São Paulo: Edições Paulinas, 1980.

LE GOFF, Jacques. O apogeu da cidade medieval. São Paulo: Martins Fontes, 2006.

LE GOFF, Jacques; SCHMITT, Jean-Claude (Org). Dicionário temático do ocidente medieval. Bauru: IIEDUSC, 2006.

LITURGIA DAS HORAS I. 3. ed. [São Paulo]: Editora Vozes; Edições Paulinas; Editora Salesiana; Dom Bosco, 1985.

MACHADO, J. C. Aparecida na história e na literatura. São Paulo: [s.n.], 1969.

MARINS, José. Maria libertadora na caminhada da Igreja. São Paulo: Editora Ave Maria, 1986.

MASCIARELLI, Michele Giulio. Maria "LA CREDENTE". In: CONVEGNI MARIANI. Maria nel Catechismo della Chiesa Cattolica. Roma: Centro de Cultura Mariana, 1993. p. 21-56.

_____. Invocações da Virgem Maria no Brasil. 6. ed. Petrópolis: Editora Vozes, 2001.

MEGALE, Nilza Botelho. Maria na religiosidade popular. São Paulo: Editora Ave Maria, 2001.

MIEGGE, Giovanni. A Virgem Maria: ensaio de história do dogma. São Paulo: Editora Vozes, 1962.

MORIN, Edgar. Para sair do século XX. Rio de Janeiro: Nova Fronteira, 1986.

NEVES, José Simõis. Origem da poesia rítmica: hinos litúrgicos, Santo Ambrósio. [S.I.]: Editora F. França Amado, 1918.

OLIVEIRA, Pedro Assis Ribeiro de. Religiões Populares. São Paulo: Paulinas, 1988. (Curso de Verão - ano II).

PAGELS, Elaine. Adão, Eva e a serpente. Rio de Janeiro: Roco, 1992.

PELIKAN, Jaroslav. Maria através dos séculos: seu papel na história da cultura. São Paulo: Companhia das Letras, 2000.

POLÓNIA, Amélia. Navegação e astronomia medieval. Revista da Faculdade de Letras e História, Porto, série III, v. 6, 2003.

RAHNER, Karl. Curso fundamental da fé. São Paulo: Paulus, 1989.

REIS, Martha dos. O culto à Senhora Aparecida: síntese entre o catolicismo oficial e o popular no Brasil. 1999. Tese (Doutorado) – Faculdade de Filosofia e Ciência, UNESP, São Paulo, 1999.

HORSLEY, Richard. The liberation of Christmas: the infancy narratives in Social Context. New York: Crossroad Publishing, 1989.

SALES, Francisco. Filotéia ou introdução à vida devota. Tradução de João José P. de Castro. Petrópolis: Editora Vozes, 2002.

SCHREINER, Klaus. De Serva do Senhor a nobre Senhora e Rainha celeste. In: _____. Maria: Virgen, Madre, Reina. Barcelona: Herder, 1996. Cap. VIII.

SILVA, Jairo José Reis da. A imagem de Maria na cidade de Duque de Caxias: mulheres católicas e a teologia da libertação. 1994. Tese (Mestrado) – Instituto Universitário de Pesquisas do Rio de Janeiro Rio de Janeiro, Universidade Cândido Mendes, Rio de Janeiro, 1994.

SOUSA, Cruz e. Poesia Completa. Florianópolis: Fundação Catarinense de Cultura; Fundação Banco do Brasil, 1993.

SOUZA, Juliana Beatriz. Mãe negra de um povo mestiço: história da devoção à Nossa Senhora da Conceição Aparecida e identidade nacional no Brasil (1717 – 1930) . Rio de Janeiro: UFF, 1996.

Sites Consulted

GABRIELLI, Fatima.Cifras e partituras.Available at: <http://www.fatimagabrielli.com.br/cifrasepartituras.php>. Access on: October 10th (2008)

JUVENTUDE MARIANA VICENTINA. Cânticos marianos. Available at: <www.jmvportugal.no.sapo.pt/musicas/canticos_marianos.html>.Access: October 10th (2008)

KOLLING, Miria Therezinha. Developed by Ir. Miria Therezinha Kolling. Available at: <www.irmamiria.com.br>.Access: October 5th (2008)

MISSIONÁRIOS CLARETIANOS. Developed by Claret. Available at: <http://www.claret.org>. Access: October 5th (2008)

ROSSI, Marcelo.Maria, mãe de todos nós. Available at: <http://mariamaedetodosnos.padremarcelorossi.letrasdemusicas.com.br/>.Access: October 5th 2008a.

_____. Nossa Senhora (mãe querida). Available at: <http://www.nossasenhoramaequerida.padremarcelorossi.letrasdemusicas.com.br/>. Access on: October 10th 2008b.

VATICANO. Developed by the Vatican. Available at: <http://www.vatican.va/archive/cathechism_po/index_new/prima-pag>. Accessed on: April 10th 2008.

Abut the Author

Graduated in Languages (Portuguese / English) at the Federal University of Mato Grosso do Sul, UFMS, and in Masters in Philology and Portuguese Language from the University of São Paulo, USP. She had received literary prizes, two of them for successful participation in the Essay Contest for Professors, organized by the Brazilian Academy of Letters (ABL) and Folha Dirigida. She was awarded with the Motion of Congratulations from the Municipal Council of Ilha Solteira, SP, by representing the city in the regional phase of the Paulista Cultural Map. She was awarded for the publication of the book entitled "II Prize of Racial Equality" organized by the SMPP/CONE.